Lecture Notes in Computer Science 11930

More information about this series at http://www.springer.com/series/7409

José Abdelnour Nocera ·
Antigoni Parmaxi · Marco Winckler ·
Fernando Loizides · Carmelo Ardito ·
Ganesh Bhutkar · Peter Dannenmann (Eds.)

Beyond Interactions

INTERACT 2019 IFIP TC 13 Workshops
Paphos, Cyprus, September 2–6, 2019
Revised Selected Papers

 Springer

Editors
José Abdelnour Nocera 🆔
University of West London
London, UK

ITI/Larsys
Funchal, Portugal

Marco Winckler 🆔
Nice Sophia Antipolis University
Sophia Antipolis, France

Carmelo Ardito 🆔
Polythecnic University of Bari
Bari, Italy

Peter Dannenmann 🆔
RheinMain University of Applied Sciences
Wiesbaden, Germany

Antigoni Parmaxi 🆔
Cyprus University of Technology
Limassol, Cyprus

Fernando Loizides 🆔
Cardiff University
Cardiff, UK

Ganesh Bhutkar
Vishwakarma Institute of Technology
Pune, India

ISSN 0302-9743   ISSN 1611-3349   (electronic)
Lecture Notes in Computer Science
ISBN 978-3-030-46539-1   ISBN 978-3-030-46540-7   (eBook)
https://doi.org/10.1007/978-3-030-46540-7

LNCS Sublibrary: SL3 – Information Systems and Applications, incl. Internet/Web, and HCI

This Springer imprint is published by the registered company Springer Nature Switzerland AG
The registered company address is: Gewerbestrasse 11, 6330 Cham, Switzerland

Foreword

This volume presents a series of revised papers selected from workshops organized by IFIP TC 13 Working Groups (WGs) during the 17th IFIP TC13 International Conference on Human-Computer Interaction, INTERACT 2019, which was held in September 2019 in Paphos, Cyprus. INTERACT 2019 was hosted by the Cyprus University of Technology (CUT) and Tallinn University. The conference was co-sponsored by the Research Centre on Interactive media, Smart systems and Emerging technologies (RISE) and Springer. It was in cooperation with ACM and ACM SIGCHI.

The contents of this volume vary from descriptions of design products to design solutions with users' needs at heart. For both researchers and designers in the field of human-computer interaction (HCI), the question is to design products and services that would have a direct impact on their users. Thus, in the era of emerging economies, HCI contributions in terms for products and services are timely and necessary. The IFIP TC 13 WGs brings together different facets of HCI with an eye to discuss practices and strategies employed by practitioners and instructional designers as well as their impact on the design of products and services.

This post-proceeding presents the outcome of a thorough and competitive selection process which started with the selection of workshops for INTERACT 2019. The IFIP TC13 WGs were challenged to propose workshops that match the main topics of the INTERACT conference. We were open to welcome workshops in diverse formats, including paper and poster presentations followed by forum discussions with participants. The selection process of workshops was juried by workshop co-chairs and members of the International Program Committee of INTERACT 2019.

Workshops preceded the main conference, running September 2–6, 2019. Only participants that submitted contributions were allowed to attend workshops. However, a dedicated session called "Workshops Summary Section" was held during the last day of INTERACT 2019 so that workshop organizers and contributors could report the outcomes of each workshop, receive comments, and interact with participants of the main conference.

Accepted workshops were allowed to establish their own reviewing process. However, to ensure the scientific quality of these post-proceedings we requested that papers selected for this volume should be peer reviewed by an international committee. After the workshop, authors were requested to revise their contributions including the comments and remarks they received during the event. Extended versions were then scrutinized again by the editors of the present volume.

The selected papers show advances in the field of HCI and they demonstrate the maturity of the work performed by IFIP TC13 WGs. We have selected 12 papers that are organized in 3 sections that correspond to IFIP TC13 workshops at INTERACT 2019.

It is important to mention that IFIP TC13 WGs are open to welcome new members. The full list of IFIP TC13 WGs is available at http://ifip-tc13.org/working-groups/ and we invite the interested readers to contact the officers for further information on how to get enrolled in WG activities such as the workshops organized at the INTERACT conference.

March 2020

José Abdelnour Nocera
Antigoni Parmaxi
Marco Winckler
Fernando Loizides
Carmelo Ardito
Ganesh Bhutkar
Peter Dannenmann

IFIP TC13 - http://ifip-tc13.org/

Established in 1989, the International Federation for Information Processing Technical Committee on Human–Computer Interaction (IFIP TC 13) is an international committee of 35 member national societies and 10 Working Groups (WGs), representing specialists of the various disciplines contributing to the field of Human-Computer Interaction (HCI). This includes (among others) human factors, ergonomics, cognitive science, computer science, and design. INTERACT is its flagship conference of IFIP TC 13, staged biennially in different countries in the world. The first INTERACT conference was held in 1984 running triennially and became a biennial event in 1993.

IFIP TC 13 aims to develop the science, technology, and societal aspects of HCI by encouraging empirical research; promoting the use of knowledge and methods from the human sciences in design and evaluation of computer systems; promoting better understanding of the relation between formal design methods and system usability and acceptability; developing guidelines, models, and methods by which designers may provide better human-oriented computer systems; and cooperating with other groups, inside and outside IFIP, to promote user-orientation and humanization in system design. Thus, TC 13 seeks to improve interactions between people and computers, to encourage the growth of HCI research and its practice in industry, and to disseminate these benefits worldwide.

The main orientation is to place the users at the center of the development process. Areas of study include: the problems people face when interacting with computers; the impact of technology deployment on people in individual and organizational contexts; the determinants of utility, usability, acceptability, and user experience; the appropriate allocation of tasks between computers and users especially in the case of automation; modeling the user, their tasks, and the interactive system to aid better system design; and harmonizing the computer to user characteristics and needs.

While the scope is thus set wide, with a tendency toward general principles rather than particular systems, it is recognized that progress will only be achieved through both general studies to advance theoretical understanding and specific studies on practical issues (e.g., interface design standards, software system resilience, documentation, training material, appropriateness of alternative interaction technologies, guidelines, the problems of integrating multimedia systems to match system needs and organizational practices, etc.).

In 2015, TC 13 approved the creation of a Steering Committee (SC) for the INTERACT conference. The SC is responsible for:

- Promoting and maintaining the INTERACT conference as the premiere venue for researchers and practitioners interested in the topics of the conference (this requires a refinement of the topics above)
- Ensuring the highest quality for the contents of the event

- Setting up the bidding process to handle the future INTERACT conferences (the decision is made up at TC 13 level)
- Providing advice to the current and future chairs and organizers of the INTERACT conference
- Providing data, tools, and documents about previous conferences to the future conference organizers
- Selecting the reviewing system to be used throughout the conference (as this impacts the entire set of reviewers)
- Resolving general issues involved with the INTERACT conference
- Capitalizing history (good and bad practices)

In 1999, TC 13 initiated a special IFIP Award, the Brian Shackel Award, for the most outstanding contribution in the form of a refereed paper submitted to and delivered at each INTERACT. The award draws attention to the need for a comprehensive human-centered approach in the design and use of information technology in which the human and social implications have been taken into account. In 2007 IFIP TC 13 also launched an Accessibility Award to recognize an outstanding contribution in HCI with international impact dedicated to the field of accessibility for disabled users. In 2013 IFIP TC 13 launched the Interaction Design for International Development (IDID) Award that recognizes the most outstanding contribution to the application of interactive systems for social and economic development of people in developing countries. Since the process to decide the award takes place after papers are sent to publisher for publication, the awards are not identified in the proceedings.

IFIP TC 13 also recognizes pioneers in the area of HCI. An IFIP TC 13 Pioneer is one who, through active participation in IFIP Technical Committees or related IFIP groups, has made outstanding contributions to the educational, theoretical, technical, commercial, or professional aspects of analysis, design, construction, evaluation, and use of interactive systems. IFIP TC 13 pioneers are appointed annually and awards are handed over at the INTERACT conference.

IFIP TC 13 stimulates working events and activities through its WGs. WGs consist of HCI experts from many countries, who seek to expand knowledge and find solutions to HCI issues and concerns within their domains. New WGs are formed as areas of significance in HCI arise.

Further information is available at the IFIP TC13 website: http://ifip-tc13.org/.

IFIP TC13 Members

Officers

Chairperson

Philippe Palanque, France

Vice-chair for Awards

Paula Kotze, South Africa

Vice-chair for Communications

Helen Petrie, UK

Vice-chair for Growth and Reach Out INTERACT Steering Committee Chair

Jan Gulliksen, Sweden

Vice-chair for Working Groups

Simone D. J. Barbosa, Brazil

Treasurer

Virpi Roto, Finland

Secretary

Marco Winckler, France

INTERACT Steering Committee Chair

Anirudha Joshi, India

Country Representatives

ACM

Gerrit van der Veer   Association for Computing Machinery, USA

Australia

Henry B. L. Duh   Australian Computer Society

Austria

Geraldine Fitzpatrick   Austrian Computer Society

Belgium

Bruno Dumas   IMEC – Interuniversity Micro-Electronics Center

Brazil

Milene Selbach Silveira   Brazilian Computer Society (SBC)

Bulgaria

Stoyan Georgiev Dentchev   Bulgarian Academy of Sciences

Canada

Lu Xiao   Canadian Information Processing Society

CLEI

Jaime Sánchez   Centro Latinoamericano de Estudios en Informatica, Chile

Croatia

Andrina Granic   Croatian Information Technology Association (CITA)

Cyprus

Panayiotis Zaphiris   Cyprus Computer Society

Czech Republic

Zdeněk Míkovec   Czech Society for Cybernetics and Informatics

Finland

Virpi Roto   Finnish Information Processing Association

France

Philippe Palanque   Société informatique de France (SIF)

Germany

Tom Gross   Gesellschaft fur Informatik e.V.

Hungary

Cecilia Sik Lanyi   John V. Neumann Computer Society

India

Anirudha Joshi   Computer Society of India (CSI)

Ireland

Liam J. Bannon   Irish Computer Society

Italy

Fabio Paternò   Italian Computer Society

Japan

Yoshifumi Kitamura   Information Processing Society of Japan

The Netherlands

Regina Bernhaupt   Nederlands Genootschap voor Informatica

New Zealand

Mark Apperley   New Zealand Computer Society

Norway

Frode Eika Sandnes   Norwegian Computer Society

Poland

Marcin Sikorski   Polish Academy of Sciences

Portugal

Pedro Campos   Associacão Portuguesa para o Desenvolvimento
                          da Sociedade da Informação (APDSI)

Serbia

Aleksandar Jevremovic   Informatics Association of Serbia

Singapore

Shengdong Zhao   Singapore Computer Society

Slovakia

Wanda Benešová   The Slovak Society for Computer Science

Slovenia

Matjaž Debevc   The Slovenian Computer Society INFORMATIKA

South Africa

Janet L. Wesson   The Computer Society of South Africa
Paula Kotze   The Computer Society of South Africa

Sweden

Jan Gulliksen   Swedish Interdisciplinary Society for Human-Computer
                             Interaction Swedish Computer Society

Switzerland

Denis Lalanne   Swiss Federation for Information Processing

Tunisia

Mona Laroussi   École Supérieure des Communications De Tunis
                             (SUP'COM)

UK

José Abdelnour Nocera   British Computer Society (BCS)

UAE

Ghassan Al-Qaimari   UAE Computer Society

Expert Members

Carmelo Ardito, Italy   Julio Abascal, Spain
Orwa, Kenya   Kaveh Bazargan, Iran
David Lamas, Estonia   Marta Kristin Larusdottir, Iceland
Dorian Gorgan, Romenia   Nikolaos Avouris, Greece
Eunice Sari, Australia/Indonesia   Peter Forbrig, Germany
Fernando Loizides, UK/Cyprus   Torkil Torkil Clemmensen, Denmark
Ivan Burmistrov, Russia   Zhengjie Liu, China

IFIP TC13 Working Groups

WG 13.1 - Education in HCI and HCI Curricula

The Working Group 13.1 aims to improve HCI education at all levels of higher education, coordinate and unite efforts to develop HCI curricula, and promote HCI teaching.

Chair

Konrad Baumann   FH Joanneum University of Applied Sciences, Austria

Vice-chairs

Jean Vanderdonckt   Université catholique de Louvain (UCL), Belgium
Carlo Giovannella   University of Rome Tor Vergata, Italy

Secretary

Konrad Baumann   FH Joanneum University of Applied Sciences, Austria

WG 13.2 - Methodologies for User-Centered System Design

The Working Group 13.2 provides an umbrella for academia researchers, students, and industry practitioners, who have an interest in fundamental theory, practices, and technology related to the user-centered design philosophy.

Chair

Marco Winckler   Université Nice Sophia Antipolis (Polytech), France

Vice-chairs

Marta Kristin Larusdottir   Reykjavik University, Iceland
Cristian Bogdan   KTH, Sweden

Secretary

Kati Kuusinen   University of Southern Denmark, Denmark

WG 13.3 - Human-Computer Interaction and Disability

The Working Group 13.3 aims to make designers of information and communications technologies and complementary tools aware of the needs of these groups in order to encourage the development of more appropriate tools for accessibility and usability. As a result, systems will become more universally accessible and the market for them will increase.

Chair

Helen Petrie   University of York, UK

Vice-chair

Gerhard Weber   Technical University Dresden, Germany

Secretary

David Sloan   University of Dundee, UK

WG 13.4/2.7 - User Interface Engineering

The Working Group 2.7/13.4 encompasses activities of the Technical Committees on Human-Computer Interaction (TC13) and Software: Theory and Practice (TC2). It aims to investigate the nature, concepts, and construction of interactive systems. Advancing the state of the art in user interface engineering and science through meetings and collaborations between researchers who are experts in the system and user aspects of the engineering design of interactive systems. Engineering emphasizes the application of scientific knowledge and rigorous structured design methods to, predictably and reliably improve the consistency, usability, scalability, economy, and dependability of practical problem solutions.

Chair

José Creissac Campos   Universidade do Minho, Portugal

Vice-chair

Gaëlle Calvary   Laboratoire d'Informatique de Grenoble, France

Secretary

Judy Bowen   University of Waikato, New Zealand

WG 13.5 - Resilience, Reliability, Safety and Human Error in System Development

The Working Group 13.5 aims to support practitioners, regulators, and researchers to develop leading edge techniques in hazard analysis and the safety engineering of computer-based systems.

Chair

Christopher Johnson   University of Glasgow, UK

Vice-chairs

Michael Feary   NASA, Ames Research Center, USA
Asaf Degani   General Motors R&D, Israel

Secretary

Philippe Palanque   ICS-IRIT, University Paul Sabatier, France

WG13.6 - Human-Work Interaction Design (HWID)

The Working Group 13.6 aims to encourage empirical studies and conceptualizations of the interaction among humans, their variegated social contexts and the technology they use both within and across these contexts. It also aims to promote the use of knowledge, concepts, methods, and techniques that enables user studies to procure a better apprehension of the complex interplay between individual, social, and organizational contexts and thereby a better understanding of how and why people work in the ways they do.

Chair

Barbara Rita Barricelli   Università degli Studi di Milano, Italy

Vice-chairs

Pedro Campos   University of Madeira, Portugal
Torkil Clemmensen   Copenhagen Business School, Denmark
José Abdelnour Nocera   University of West London, UK and ITI/Larsys, Portugal
Arminda Guerra Lopes   Polytechnic Institute of Castelo Branco, Portugal
Dinesh Katre   Centre for Development of Advanced Computing, India

Secretary

Frederica Gonçalves   University of Madeira, Portugal

WG 13.7 - Human-Computer Interaction and Visualization (HCIV)

The Working Group 13.7 aims to provide a creative work environment for performing innovative research at the interface between Human-Computer Interaction and Visualization.

Chair

Peter Dannenmann   RheinMain University of Applied Sciences, Germany

Vice-chairs

Gerrit van der Veer   Association for Computing Machinery (ACM), USA
Nahum Gershon   The MITRE Corporation, USA

Secretary

Achim Ebert   University of Kaiserslautern, Germany

WG 13.8 - Interaction Design and International Development

The aims of the Working Group 13.8 is to support and develop the research, practice, and education capabilities of HCI in institutions and organizations based around the world taking into account their diverse local needs and cultural perspectives.

Chair

José Abdelnour Nocera   University of West London, UK and ITI/Larsys, Portugal

Vice-chairs

Andy Dearden   Sheffield Hallam University, UK
Torkil Clemmensen   Copenhagen Business School, Denmark
Christian Sturm   Hamm-Lippstadt University of Applied Sciences, Germany

Secretary

Anirudha Joshi   IIT Bombay, India

WG 13.9 - Interaction Design and Children

The Working Group 13.9 aims to support practitioners, regulators, and researchers to develop the study of interaction design and children across international contexts.

Chair

Janet Read   University of Central Lancashire, UK

Vice-chair

Panos Markopoulos   Eindhoven University of Technology, The Netherlands

Secretary

Matthew Horton   University of Central Lancashire, UK

WG 13.10 - Human-Centred Technology for Sustainability

The Working Group 13.10 aims to promote research, design, development, evaluation, and deployment of human-centered technology to encourage sustainable use of resources in various domains. These technologies would include interaction techniques, interfaces, and visualizations for applications, tools, games, services, and devices.

Chair

Masood Masoodian   Aalto University, Finland

Vice-chairs

Elisabeth André   Augsburg University, Germany
Nuno J. Nunes   University of Madeira, Portugal

Secretary

Thomas Rist   University of Applied Sciences Augsburg, Germany

Workshops Organized by IFIP TC13 Working Groups at INTERACT 2019

Workshop Jointly Organized by Working Group 13.2 and Working Group 13.5

Workshop on Handling Security, Usability, User Experience and Reliability in User-Centered Development Processes

Carmelo Ardito	Politecnico di Bari, Italy
Regina Bernhaupt	Eindhoven University of Technology, The Netherlands
Philippe Palanque	Université Paul Sabatier, France
Stefan Sauer	Paderborn University, Germany

Website: https://sites.google.com/site/ifipwg132workshopinteract19/home

Workshop Organized by Working Group 13.6

User Experiences and Wellbeing at Work (UX@Work)

Ganesh Bhutkar	Vishwakarma Institute of Technology (VIT) Pune, India
Virpi Roto	Aalto University, Finland
Pedro Campos	Madeira Interactive Technologies Institute (M-iti), Portugal
Torkil Clemmensen	Copenhagen Business School, Denmark
Alexander Meschtscherjakov	Salzburg University, Austria
Barbara Rita Barricelli	Università degli Studi di Milano, Italy
José Abdelnour Nocera	University of West London, UK and ITI/Larsys, Portugal
Arminda Lopes	Madeira Interactive Technologies Institute (M-iti), Portugal
Frederica Gonçalves	Madeira Interactive Technologies Institute (M-iti), Portugal

Website: https://blogs.aalto.fi/uxatwork/

Workshop Organized by Working Group 13.7

Beyond Computers: Wearables, Humans, and Things - WHAT!

Organizers

Gerrit van der Veer	Association for Computing Machinery (ACM), USA
Achim Ebert	University of Kaiserslautern, Germany
Nahum Gershon	The MITRE Corporation, USA
Peter Dannenmann	RheinMain University of Applied Sciences, Germany

Website: http://www.hciv.de/what19/index.html

Sponsors and Partners

Sponsors

Partners

International Federation for Information Processing

TALLINN UNIVERSITY

In-cooperation with ACM   In-cooperation with SIGCHI

Contents

Beyond Computers: Wearables, Humans, and Things - WHAT!

Supporting the Experience of Stakeholders of Multimedia Art – Towards an Ontology

Danzhu Li[1,2(✉)] and Gerrit C. van der Veer[2,3]

[1] Human Media Interaction, University Twente, Enschede, The Netherlands
lidanzhu@me.com
[2] Multimedia and Animation, Luxun Academy of Fine Arts, Liaoning, China
gerrit@acm.org
[3] Multimedia and Culture, Computer Science, Vrije Universiteit, Amsterdam, The Netherlands

Abstract. We introduce the rapid change of the visual art ecosystem, triggered by current science and technology development. ICT enables new multimedia based an interactive art forms, with an increasing variety of stakeholders. We provide examples of audience involvement, of immersion, and of brain-computer interaction as a new paradigm for participation. We point to the use of new material dimensions, as well as to expanding shared creation and cognition. We also point to opportunities to apply this development to accommodate special needs. In order to support the dissemination of these possibilities, we advocate the development of a task-modeling based ontology to describe, analyse, and support the evolving art ecosystem.

Keywords: Contemporary visual art ecosystem · Stakeholders · Ontology

1 Visual Art on the Move

Our profession includes to support modern art, i.e., to teach, and to publish, relevant knowledge and skills to participate in the current and future art ecosystem. For the various stakeholders, the relevant view will be different, but stakeholders need to collaborate and communicate so a common language is needed that supports an intuitive cultural base. We are aiming on that and we intend to discuss this with the workshop/panel.

From ancient times, innovation of tools and techniques did push art to a new level. But today, with ICT, dramatic changes occur everywhere, including in the world of visual arts. Rich media, as well as information visualization, became a common way of modern visual communication, and these interact with each other.

We have been exploring how contemporary artists are modifying the relationship between human beings and new realities. This will lead to an expansion of the multi-dimensional concept of experience, including the notion of values of visual art for its different stakeholders.

This paper analyses the current situation and developing trends of contemporary visual art from the perspective of enriching all stakeholders' experience, which suggests

© IFIP International Federation for Information Processing 2020
Published by Springer Nature Switzerland AG 2020
J. Abdelnour Nocera et al. (Eds.): INTERACT 2019, LNCS 11930, pp. 3–15, 2020.
https://doi.org/10.1007/978-3-030-46540-7_1

that contemporary visual artists should be aware. Through observation, practice, interviews and other research methods, we analyze and study the development and changes of the work and survival of stakeholders in contemporary visual (mainly interactive) art. Contemporary visual arts move to a cross disciplinary or interdisciplinary context, related to the development of science and technology and the change of human aesthetic ability. A new type of cross-border artists is coming out, and the evolution of society will make the space of art broader, evolving to a new visual art ecology.

2   Different Experiences Brought by Science and Technology

Under the influence of science and technology, new forms of art have emerged. These new terms may be controversial, but their names do reflect a future trend of contemporary art: digital art; interactive art; technique art; generative art; bio art; and singularity art [1].

We observed that visual art in due time approaches motion art. In relation to this, the operations of the artists and performers changed, including a gradual transfer from mainly perceptual motor skill activities to cognitive activities, gradually including application of ICT. It urges us to predict the short-term future of art, based on our collection and collation of long-term historic technology-related information.

Contemporary dynamic visual art is oriented towards integrated media, the involvement of science and technology, and interactive, cross-border, multi-disciplinary cooperation. We predict that in the short term, art will go through a period where the practical value is greater than the aesthetic value. We analyze the impact and reflect on the changes and demands of experience and on the different levels of values from a cognitive perspective.

3   Interactive Media Are Multi-dimensional

Modern visual art has developed to the interactive stage, resembling the development of HCI (human-computer interaction) technology. Artists explore the possibilities of interaction between human beings and machines, as well as between machines. Due to the rapid development of mobiles and wearable devices, interactive art features in a multi-dimensional context, serving a multi-sensory experience.

The change of experience elicits artists and audiences to co-create. The continuous improvement of technology has a direct relationship with the impact of artistic creation. Consequently, artists need to understand and learn to use new technologies.

Interactive media art based on virtual reality and augmented reality is becoming to a major form of contemporary visual art innovation. From the commercialization of tools, to the development of models, to the sharing of various open-source information platforms, artists are becoming more familiar with this performance form and are as devoted as their audience. Mixed Reality technology enables participants (artists and spectators) to extend their experience in the dimension of time and space, breaking the old way of appreciation. We will provide some examples:

Fig. 1. a. Character for the game DNF (2018). Picture by the authors, Dalian, China. **b.** The game DNF created with shadow play techniques (2018). Picture by the authors, Dalian, China.

3.1   Chinese Artists Play with Their Audiences

XuanPin, "The Field", is a comprehensive media art work. The work is intended to celebrate the tenth anniversary of the birth of a game DNF, created by LAFA [2] teachers and students, the Tencent Company, and Chinese folk artists.

Based on the ancient shadow play, this work combines shadow play with animation and laser printing, MR immersion interaction, and other comprehensive media. It triggers people to think about tradition and modern art and technology.

In order to let young people know about traditional culture, the team applied the latest Halo lens hybrid reality technology to interpret the scenes and images in DNF games and show them in the form of shadow play. In this arena, audiences can watch the performances of non-hereditary artists, and experience the performances made with new materials by players of cosplay roles, and, in addition, take HoloLens glasses to watch and try the performance of the shadows in virtual scenes.

This multi-dimensional interaction is an innovation and exploration of traditional visual art. Figure 1 shows the character designed in the game DNF, created with shadow play techniques. Figure 2 shows Cosplay actor performance in the game by using shadow play, where the audience manipulates the shadow puppet in the virtual scene through HoloLens. One of the authors participated in the creation.

3.2   Lie Down and Enjoy Arts - Immersion Experience

Both authors participated in the Art exhibition of SIGCHI2018, lying down on the floor to experience the art and enjoying it.

Figure 3 shows one of the works. In the exhibition hall, artists built a dome theatre with dozens of cushions on the floor. Under the half dome, audiences had to lie down to see the dynamic visual art projected on the inside of the dome. In Fig. 3 we can see a Korean artist playing with instruments and electric fans moving under the dome. At the same time, they were "projected" into the dome.

This combination became a rich comprehensive performance. Obviously, artists have broken the traditional form of experience, like under the domes of ancient churches or palaces in Europe. The artists challenge the audience's experience to complete their co-creation and to become part of this dynamic artistic performance.

3.3   Life Information Visualization - Brain-Computer Interface Art

The history of BCI as an artistic means is still short. Current BCI for artistic creation is mainly the application of non - invasive systems (EEG) to ensure a safe and noninvasive experience for artists and viewers. The brain signals picked up by electrodes are sent to the computer, which uses sophisticated software to translate them into computer commands.

Portability and relatively low prices make the technology easy to promote. In this way, the audience can participate in the dynamics of the art without physical actions on the piece of art, and can even co-create, either individually or (when appropriately designed by the artist) as a group of spectators. This is the embodiment and the charm

Fig. 2. Cosplay actors' performance of the DNF game by using shadow play and the audience manipulating the shadow puppet in the virtual scene through HoloLens. Picture provided by Media and Animation college, LAFA.

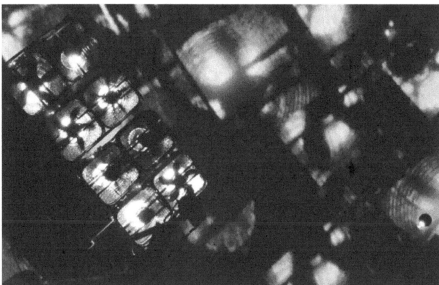

Fig. 3. Art exhibition, SIGCHI 2018, Montreal. Picture by the authors.

of BCI in an aesthetic application, which changes the form of traditional art and of the appreciation (no longer restricted to an objective perspective).

Obviously, contemporary artists need to understand the changing perspective on the role of the audience, as well as the technical aspects of designing the interaction, to apply this in their creation. Figure 4 shows scientists using Mobile Brain-body Imaging (MoBI) technology to study the human improvisational creative process in the spirit of

Fig. 4. Exquisite Corpse – Visual Arts, http://uhbmi.ee.uh.edu/portfolio/ec-m-2/

the "Exquisite Corpse" (an improvisational creative game created by surrealists in the 1920s, where three artists create a three-part art piece). The performance-study seeks to uncover clues to what happens in the brain as people create and contemplate art [3].

4   Opportunities and Challenges Faced by Artists in Their Exploration of Materials

The development of art is accompanied by the use of different materials and tools. In modern society, with highly developed science and Internet, artists' exploration of new materials closely follows the pace of science and technology, though limited by the development of materials and technology. In this process, we can see that the symbiotic fields of art and technology affect each other, which catalyzes the innovation of art ecology.

According to the authors' long-term observation, a new group is gradually growing in the contemporary visual art ecology. They have subverted the public's traditional understanding of art. They generally have multiple identities or skills. Their backgrounds are computer scientists, material scientists, engineers and even biologists. We have noticed this in our early research on the art stakeholders, and we have continuously tracked the development and change of this group. We have analyzed that the development of modern education supports contemporary artists to have rich knowledge, combined with a scientific development concept and methodology.

Because of the growing number of artists with comprehensive qualities, the art market is increasingly dynamic, making the exhibition more diversified, and the audience's experience more and more multidimensional. With the improvement of the public's aesthetic level, this promotes the artists' thinking and change. Furthermore, as the interaction between the audience and art becomes more and more active, it promotes the development of cross-border artists.

We understand that they (artists and art works) blur the boundary between art and technology. But there is a real controversy. We predict that, in the near future, this group will continue to expand which will inevitably affect the development of the next generation of artists, and will update human cognition of art. We must consider both sides of the development of things.

4.1 A Plea for the Role of Material Science Development

An increasing number of artists focus on interaction mechanisms with wearable and implantable devices as well as integrating Internet-of-Things technology with new interactive art paradigms. In fact, both artists and scientists are aiming at a substance between visible and invisible. With the development of material science, new artistic forms such as nano-art, bio-art and integrated material art have brought challenges to those avant-garde artists in exploring future art. Though many mainstream artists and stakeholders turn a blind eye, or lack foresight, to the rapid development of contemporary science and technology, some artists are exploring the humanization of technology. New materials like nanomaterials are expected to be widely used in future artistic creation. Today we may already witness contemporary artistic practices in this direction. For example, nano-printing art, nano-sculpture, and nano-animation:

Jonty Hurwitz's work "The FRAGILE GIANT" (Fig. 5) on animal protection is the smallest nano-sculpture in history. In this microcosmic world, the artist explores the relationship between man and nature. This elephant sculpture is just over on tenth of a millimeter high. It is walking along the stark and perilous landscape of a human fingerprint. It can be destroyed by a human breath. According to Hurwitz the sculptures are so tiny that they are invisible to the human eye, and able to be placed on the forehead of an ant. Details of the works are at 300-nm scale, similar to the wavelengths of visible light and are therefore nearly impossible, according to the laws of physics, to see in the visible spectrum. The only way to observe these works is through a non-optical method of magnification like a scanning electron microscope [4].

IBM Research claimed to make the "World's Smallest Movie Using Atoms" (Fig. 6). IBM took the challenge of moving 5,000 atoms around in order to create a short stop motion video, capturing the images using a scanning tunneling microscope. "A Boy and His Atom" depicts a character named Atom who befriends a single atom and goes on a playful journey that includes dancing, playing catch and bouncing on a trampoline. Set to a playful musical track, the movie represents a unique way to convey science outside the research community [5].

Technology turns inspiration and creativity into reality, challenging traditional thinking and bringing about an art revolution, and even triggering to build a new world view. This innovation requires collaboration between many different interdisciplinary experts. The cooperation and co-creation will generate a new cognitive system (a symbiotic relationship between human beings' wearables, and the context). Wearable devices may have powerful effect on our experience of the context, of interactive art, and of life. Smart fabric in wearable devices is a representative case. Sensors are becoming smaller (to nanoscale units), and smart fabric applications become more flexible and comfortable [6]. Artists' exploration of science and art has stimulated people's re-recognition of the reality of contemporary art.

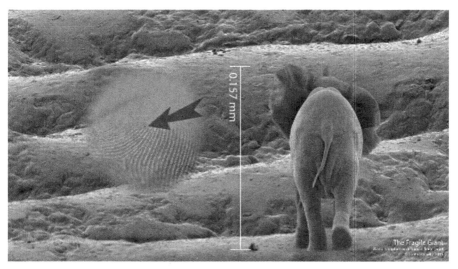

Fig. 5. Jonty Hurwitz: "*THE FRAGILE GIANT*". The smallest man-made object ever to be filmed (2015). https://jontyhurwitz.com/fragile-giant

4.2 Appealing to Contemporary Visual Art Ecology to Keep Pace with the Times

The workshop theme "Information Retrieved from (large) WHAT Networks" (INTER-ACT 2019, Cyprus) has inspired us to think about Privacy issued have to be considered (copyright, personal data of audience…), and information security, human rights and ethical disputes. It is essential for building a sound and beautiful future art ecology. This chapter is therefore extended. We are concerned about two aspects:

a. based on the era of the Internet of things, digital art copyright issues and works related to the collection and use of biological information security issues. and
b. with the application of life science and material science to artists' creation, some controversies have touched on the rights and moral disputes of human beings, animals and other livings, such as "The Vacanti Mouse": Twenty years ago, Harvard surgeons Joseph and his brother Charles Vacanti, along with MIT engineer Bob Langer, experimented with techniques to create human body parts in the lab. They implanted the shape of a human ear in the back of a mouse [7]. Some people regard it as an artistic act, which has aroused controversy.

Again, the contemporary artwork named Sugababe (Exhibited in ZKM in 2014) is a Bio-Sculpture by Diemut Strebe (Fig. 7). A living bioengineered replica of Vincent van Gogh's ear grown from tissue engineered cartilage cells procured from a direct male descendant and containing natural genetic information about Vincent as well as genetically engineered components amongst using genome editing CRISPRCas9 technique, and recent bioprinting technology. One can speak to the ear through a microphone system. The input sound is connected to a computer processor, using a software program to generate simulated nerve impulses from the sound signal in real time. This mimics sound recorded from an electrode inserted into the auditory nerve, when firing [8].

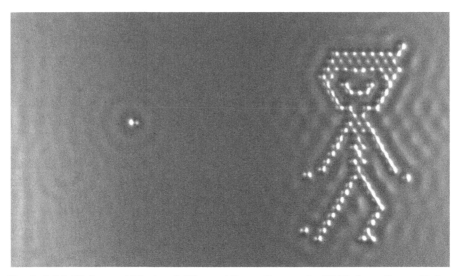

Fig. 6. IBM: "*A Boy and His Atom*". The world's smallest movie (2013). https://www-03.ibm.com/press/us/en/photo/40982.wss

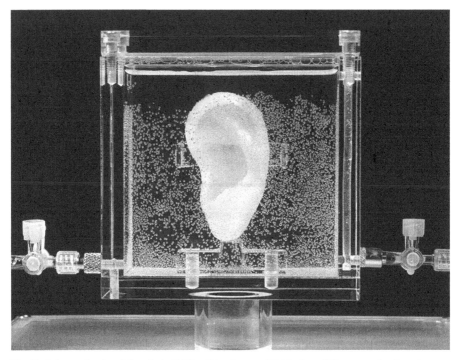

Fig. 7. Diemut Strebe: "*Sugababe*". The 3D print ear (2014). http://diemutstrebe.altervista.org

This is considered to be a representative contemporary art exploration of life science. At present, artists who can use advanced science and technology such as life science, gene technology and so on are few and far between. We explore this topic to arouse stakeholders' thoughts on future ecological development. There is no doubt that science enables artists to enter a new era in the use of materials. We not only look forward to the development of art diversity, but also consider moral constraints and legal protection.

We try and practice scientific methodology and models to build a vision of future art ecology. Cognitive Science (Sect. 5) and task modeling (Sect. 6) are the methods we are studying and practicing. We hope more and more stakeholders will pay attention to this research.

5   Exploration of Cognition

For all stakeholders of visual art, the improvement of knowledge is accompanied by the development of technology, by interdisciplinary cooperation, lifelong learning, and the application advanced technology and machine learning to assist artistic creation. Candy and Edmonds [9, 10] mention three categories of activities in the creative person's thinking and working practice were identified: knowledge, visualization, and collaboration. The quality of the type of collaboration can be assessed in terms of its durability and stimulus to creative thinking as well as the outcomes achieved.

From brush to electronic pen; from clay and stone to 3D printing: artists need to master the accessibility of technology; need to learn to use new technology for creation. Tools should meet artists' needs, and be easy to learn and use, as well as be timely updated and upgraded to meet new needs. With the development of personal computing and the coming of the era of Internet of Everything, we foresee that customized tools will serve more and more artists and stakeholders of art.

We call for the exploration and development of cognitive ergonomics in a broader scope and the application of cooperation in the field of art [11]. This includes the special community of artists with special needs. In our practice, one graduate student from the art school (LAFA) in China is a hearing-impaired artist. He is very distressed by his limitation. He worries that if he always makes silent films, he will lose audiences and his works will be excluded from the art market. At present, he can only rely on the production of silent films to solve the problem of production. This case is representative of a considerable group of artists. In combination with our participation in the Artistic BCI workshop at CHI in Montreal in 2018, we analyzed the possibility of future support for hearing-impaired artists to edit music through EEG or other bioinformatics technologies [12]. Similarly, visually impaired artists and artists with language barriers can be assisted in their creation. We currently consider Ear Touch, a one-handed interaction technique that allows visually impaired people to interact with a smartphone using the ear to tap or draw gestures on the touchscreen, facilitating one-handed use as an alternative to headphones and addressing privacy and social concerns [13]. A smart glove can already work out what the wearer is manipulating from its weight and shape [14].

6   An Ontology of Modern Visual Art

When applying ICT, artists revise the way they work. We observe that contemporary interactive art is an artistic act co-created by artists and participants. We briefly review its production process: from the manufacturing stage, artists need to cooperate with participants in many disciplines (using brainstorming, sketching, technology and tools, exhibition forms, interactive models, etc.). After completion of the artwork, it is expected to be co-creative with audience, e.g., through recording the behavior of the experiencer, visualizing the emotional information and the interactive behaviors needed. The stronger the participation, the higher the experiential value.

This is precisely the purpose of some artists 'creation: the value of such works of art. We envision an ontology to analyse, describe, and support the future art ecosystem: with new roles, new objects, and new activities.

Our conceptual framework is based on GTA [15], and we mainly consider to focus on development of the concepts Roles (with mandating and delegation), Objects (including tangible and intangible artifacts, and the context as an object), Tasks (as goal-triggered activities of (co-)creation, performance, and experiencing); and the multidisciplinary concept of values and forces that trigger action.

- **Objects** of art, both intangible (scripts, programs, video and sound streams) and tangible. Each may well have an electronic identity, with possible tags regarding ownership, location, history of use and movement.
- Stakeholders are the various **Agents** in the art ecosystem: artist; supporters of techniques and tools; stage keepers, museums and gallery owners; brokers and auction houses; performers and actors; and the audience.
- Roles. In the art ecosystem, collaboration between people (and other agents) changes: new roles develop (co-creating members of the audience) and roles get exchanged more easily between actors, activities get more easily delegated to systems, and mandating of roles and delegation of activities occurs at a more detailed level than before.
- Each agent will have one or more different **roles** (defined by **goals**, and related sets of **activities** regarding art objects), and each role will relate to different types of experience (including: understanding; emotions; tendencies to act; values toward the piece of art).
- **Activities** with their **goals** will be related to creation; reproduction; performance; exhibition; ownership and maintenance; documentation and communication about; etc.

Our analysis will allow us to set design goals for supporting technology. A new addition contribution to GTA is exploration and research of experience and values. We decide to add values aspect for the case of art, based on observing the impact of values in the current art ecosystem on artists, art markets, audiences, buyers, and other stakeholders.

With the rise and development of industry, art is gradually industrialized, which is representative of film and television animation. The film industry is a complete industrial chain. The embodiment of aesthetic value is only one of the links, though it is the most basic. After the production and distribution of films, value is still fermenting. If the cultural value and aesthetic value of a film have a broad and lasting influence, then its collection value, commercial value and other values will change with time. This phenomenon is not only controlled by the art market. Artists and agents should think about how to create valuable art, and our expanding task analysis ontology is intended to provide a scientific theory and practical tool that can help artist and stakeholders.

References

1. Qin Tan, L.: Singularity Art - How Technology Singularity Will Impact Art. China Machine Press, Beijing (2018)
2. LuXun academy of fine arts (LAFA), China. http://www.lumei.edu.cn
3. Exquisite Corpse – Visual Arts. http://uhbmi.ee.uh.edu/portfolio/ec-m-2/
4. Hurwitz, J.: The Fragile Giant - The smallest man-made object ever to be filmed (2015). https://jontyhurwitz.com/fragile-giant
5. IBM: A Boy and His Atom - The world's smallest movie (2013). https://www-03.ibm.com/press/us/en/photo/40982.wss
6. Li, D., van der Veer, G.: From painter to interaction designer: the evolution of visual art things. In: Joshi, A., Balkrishan, D., Dalvi, G., Winckler, M. (eds.) Adjunct Proceedings INTERACT 2017, Mumbai, pp. 139–149. Springer (2017)
7. Hugo, K.: Newsweek: Exclusive: Whatever Happened to the Mouse With the Ear on Its Back? (2017). https://www.newsweek.com/tissue-surgeon-ear-mouse-human-organs-transplant-cell-phones-666082
8. Diemut Strebe: Sugababe (2014). http://diemutstrebe.altervista.org
9. Candy, L.: Computers and creativity support: knowledge, visualization and collaboration. Knowl. Based Syst. **10**(1), 3–13 (1997)
10. Candy, L., Edmonds, E.A.: Modeling co-creativity in art and technology. In: Proceedings 4th Conference on Creativity & Cognition, Loughborough, United Kingdom (2002). https://dblp.uni-trier.de/db/conf/candc/candc2002.html
11. Li, D., van der Veer, G.C.: Cognitive ergonomics on the move. In: ECCE 2019 workshop, UK (2019)
12. Nijholt, A. (ed.): Brain Art: Brain-computer Interfaces for Artistic Expression. Springer, Switzerland (2019). https://doi.org/10.1007/978-3-030-14323-7
13. Wang, U., Yu, C., Yang, X.D., He, W., Shi, Y.: EarTouch: facilitating smartphone use for visually impaired people in mobile and public scenarios. In: CHI 2019. ACM Digital Library (2019)
14. Smart glove works out what you are holding from its weight and shape. Nature (2019). https://doi.org/10.1038/s41586-019-1234-z. https://www.newscientist.com/article/2204736-smart-glove-works-out-what-youre-holding-from-its-weight-and-shape/
15. Van der Veer, G.C., Kulyk, O., Vyas, D., Kubbe, O., Ebert, A.: Task modeling for collaborative authoring. In: Dittmar, A., Forbrig, P. (eds.) Designing Collaborative Activities - Proceedings of ECCE 2011, pp. 171–178. ACM Digital Library (2011)

User Experiences and Wellbeing at Work (UX@Work)

Wellbeing at Work: Four Perspectives on What User Experiences with Artifacts May Contribute

Morten Hertzum[(⊠)] [iD]

University of Copenhagen, Copenhagen, Denmark
hertzum@hum.ku.dk

Abstract. Most work involves the use of artifacts; thus, user experience (UX) is a factor in how most employees experience their work. This study revisits the tool, media, dialogue-partner, and system perspectives on artifact use to explore how UX may contribute to wellbeing at work. It is found that artifacts foster positive UX when they lend the user expressive power (tool), are transparent (media) or perceptive (dialogue partner). They foster negative UX when they break the user's task focus or make the user a mere system component. These findings are discussed and refined by elaborating the classic concepts of ready to hand and present at hand.

Keywords: Perspectives on artifact use · User experience · Wellbeing · Work

1 Introduction

Wellbeing at work [2, 4] is a major concern for employees as well as organizations because it is central to employees' mental and physical health and because it influences their productivity. Fisher [6] conceptualizes wellbeing at work as consisting of hedonic wellbeing (e.g., job satisfaction and positive affect), eudaimonic wellbeing (e.g., engagement, meaning, and intrinsic motivation), and social wellbeing (e.g., quality connections, satisfaction with coworkers, and social support). This conceptualization makes it apparent that a vast array of concrete organizational circumstances enter into shaping wellbeing at work. One of them is the employees' use of artifacts.

In the research community of human-computer interaction, the experiences associated with the use of artifacts are discussed under the rubric of user experience (UX). While multiple UX definitions have been proposed, they share a focus on the experiences associated with artifact use. For example, Roto et al. [18, p. 6] state that "UX is a subset of experience as a general concept. UX is more specific, since it is related to the experiences of using a system." Some definitions restrict UX to actual system use [3], others include anticipated use [13], and still others also include aesthetics [10]. These differences appear, however, minor compared to the shared focus on the experiences associated with artifact use. Well-documented experiences with computer artifacts in work settings include burnout, deskilling, frustration, and helplessness [e.g., 7, 16]. Countering such negative experiences is central to employee wellbeing. Replacing them with positive experiences would be an even nobler design goal.

© IFIP International Federation for Information Processing 2020
Published by Springer Nature Switzerland AG 2020
J. Abdelnour Nocera et al. (Eds.): INTERACT 2019, LNCS 11930, pp. 19–25, 2020.
https://doi.org/10.1007/978-3-030-46540-7_2

In one of the relatively few studies of UX in a work context, Meneweger et al. [17] show that ordinary user experiences dominate in factory employees' interactions with technology. The interactions are generally mundane, unremarkable, and shaped by routine activities. At the same time, studies of technology acceptance find that perceived enjoyment, a concept similar to UX, predicts the intention to use an artifact as strongly as do perceived usefulness and perceived ease of use [12]. While enjoyment contributes to hedonic wellbeing, usefulness contributes to eudaimonic wellbeing; ease of use facilitates both hedonic and eudaimonic wellbeing by reducing the effort that must be expended to obtain them. Thus, replacing ordinary user experiences with positive user experiences stands to improve employees' attitude toward the artifacts they use as well as to improve their wellbeing at work. The relation between the artifact and the user's experience is, however, complex because UX is not determined by the artifact alone. Rather, UX results from the interrelations among the characteristics of the artifact, user, task, and context of use.

While it is a largely trivial observation that UX results from the interrelations among the artifact, user, task, and context of use, it raises the question of whether artifacts as such exert much influence on wellbeing at work. It may well be that wellbeing at work is first and foremost driven by other factors, such as the task content, division of labor, physical work conditions, psychosocial climate, and decision-making influence. These factors are not directly about artifacts and, thereby, not directly about UX. To explore what we might accomplish by designing for good UX at work, this study revisits Kammersgaard's [15] four perspectives on human-computer interaction, ponders what constitutes positive and negative UX within each perspective, and discusses the possible contributions of UX to wellbeing at work.

2 Four Perspectives on System Use and UX

Kammersgaard [15] outlines four perspectives on human-computer interaction by distinguishing between artifacts for individual and collaborative use and between artifacts for which agency rests with the user and artifacts that split agency between user and artifact. The four perspectives are the tool perspective, the system perspective, the dialogue-partner perspective, and the media perspective, see Table 1.

The tool perspective has its roots in craftwork and emphasizes that in the hands of a skilled user the tool is a seamless extension of the user, who attends to her task rather than to the tool: When hammering the skilled user's attention is on driving the nail, not on the hammer. Conceptually, the tool is said to be ready to hand [9]. It is only upon breakdowns that the tool becomes the focus of the user's attention – becomes present at hand. If the hammer is too light for the size of nail or otherwise inadequate for the task then the user's attention shifts from the task to the tool. These shifts are associated with frustration and other negative emotions because the breakdown thwarts progress on the task, at least temporarily. It appears that tools foster good experiences when they are out of mind – ready to hand – and poor experiences when they become present at hand. If we take the focus on artifact use in the UX definitions to mean that the user must, in the moment, be conscious that she is using an artifact then the tool perspective rules out positive UX. The positive experiences do not qualify as UX because they are

Table 1. Four perspectives on system use, adapted from Kammersgaard [15].

	Individual	Collaborative
User agency	*Tool perspective* • Artifact is an extension of the user's body • Ready to hand vs present at hand • UX?: expressive power	*Media perspective* • Users communicate through the artifact • Media richness vs common ground • UX?: transparency, structure
Split agency	*Dialogue-partner perspective* • Artifact displays human-like behavior • Intelligent vs annoying assistant • UX?: perceptive, adaptive	*System perspective* • User is similar to other system components • Automation vs meaningful jobs • UX?: deskilling, monotony

associated with an uninterrupted focus on the task (note that this point will be modified in Sect. 3). In contrast, the user is conscious of the artifact when it thwarts task progress; thus tools can foster negative UX. If we do not require that the user must, in the moment, be conscious that she is using an artifact – and this is probably the more sensible option – then positive UX is possible within the tool perspective and consists of designing for readiness to hand. The user may however not attribute the positive UX to the tool but, partly or wholly, to other aspects of the use situation.

The system perspective aligns with industrial perceptions of work and promotes a view in which a system consists of components that may be human or automated. Each component is characterized by the inputs it receives, the activities it performs on those inputs, and the outputs it delivers. The division of the system into components is made by management and defines a division of labor. To perform their work, the users need only know the characteristics of the component they embody. Performance is measured by how cheaply, quickly, and consistently the components deliver their outputs. That is, the users' work is measured in the same way as that of the automated components. If the users perform poorer than an automated version of the same component then the users are at risk of being replaced by such an automated component. In this sense the users are measured by their ability to function as automated components. The automation inherent in the system perspective is often associated with deskilling of the users, who become operators of machines that perform more and more components of the work [1]. This negative UX results from a primary focus on automation, thereby leaving the users with the components that have not yet been automated. To create positive UX, it is necessary to focus on creating meaningful and rewarding human components, for example by automating the parts of work that are monotonous or unhealthy. However, to create meaningful and rewarding human components it may also be necessary to reconsider the separation between a managerial level that defines the components and an operational level that merely performs according to these preset definitions. That is, it may be necessary to challenge the essence of the system perspective.

The dialogue-partner perspective sees the artifact as an intelligent assistant with which the users can interact in much the same way as they interact with humans. The intelligent assistant empowers the user by serving his or her needs and does so without requiring that the user learns special commands for interacting with the assistant. Unlike the system perspective, which tends to reduce humans to machines, the dialogue-partner perspective seeks to elevate machines to human-like performance. Unlike the tool perspective, which involves the user's moment-to-moment handling of the tool, the intelligent assistant acts autonomously in the user's service. The intelligent assistant may, for example, monitor an architect's work on a building and inform the architect when his current building design violates formal regulations or recognized principles for good design [5]. The intelligent assistant fosters positive and negative UX in much the same way as a human collaborator. Negative UX ensues if the assistant needs too many instructions, performs poor work, or delivers its work at inopportune moments. Positive UX ensues if the assistant is effective and efficient and, especially, if the assistant also picks up on the tacit conditions for good performance and reacts appropriately to dynamic changes in the environment. Often, intelligent assistants must be supervised by users who need to be ready to take over in situations the assistant cannot handle. This creates poor conditions for positive UX because the user wants to offload the task to the assistant but must, instead, "stay in the loop" to be ready to step in whenever needed.

The media perspective positions the artifact as a medium through which the users interact with each other. That is, the medium is merely a channel; agency rests with the users. Rich media [19] provide for simultaneous interactions in multiple modalities and, thereby, for back-channeling (e.g., nods and raised eyebrows) to occur via some modalities at the same time as the main interaction occupies other modalities (e.g., speech). Thereby, rich media support users in establishing, sustaining, and repairing common ground, which is key to effective collaborative interactions. Conversely, lean media provide few or only a single modality and may be restricted to asynchronous interactions, thereby increasing the risk of breakdowns in common ground. Media provide positive UX when they are transparent – somewhat similar to when a tool is ready to hand. A transparent medium allows the interactions among the users to flow without distortions. Rich media are transparent with respect to more interaction modalities than lean media. In addition to transparency, some media aim to provide positive UX by structuring the interaction, for example by making explicit that an interactional turn is a request and therefore must be answered by accepting, declining or negotiating the request [21]. Media foster negative UX when they are insufficiently transparent or enforce a structure that is too rigid. In both cases the medium gets in the way of the interactions among the users.

3 Discussion

Most work involves the use of artifacts, such as products, systems or services. Thus, UX is a factor in how most employees experience their work. In the tool and media perspectives, an artifact fosters positive UX by not attracting the user's attention, which instead remains on the task. That is, it is by supporting the user in expressing her skills – as manifested in high-quality work task products – that tools and media foster positive UX. Seen from these perspectives, positive UX is about *lending the user expressive power*. In the dialogue-partner perspective, positive UX is as much about how well the artifact engages in the process of its use as it is about the product that results from this process.

That is, an artifact fosters positive UX if it is a *perceptive and adaptive dialogue partner*. In the system perspective, positive UX appears to be secondary to other concerns. That is, to foster positive UX it is necessary to *abandon the system perspective* or, at least, supplement it with other perspectives. Abandoning the system perspective is a daunting undertaking because this perspective permeates much thinking about how to organize workplaces. For example, physicians are increasingly frustrated that they spend still more of their time documenting their work in electronic patient records and comparatively less time with patients, but the increasing documentation requirements are justified by pointing out that the physician is a component in a much larger system, which needs the documentation for hospital-level quality assurance, national performance indicators, and international healthcare research [7]. This system-perspective thinking is, however, creating frustration and burnout among the physicians because it disregards the personal level from which they experience the electronic patient records.

A less ambitious goal than fostering positive UX in the service of wellbeing at work would be to avoid negative UX. The tool and media perspectives agree that artifacts foster negative UX whenever they attract the user's attention. Thus, users become conscious of their artifact use when they experience problems with the artifacts. The distinction between, on the one hand, positive UX and a task focus and, on the other hand, negative UX and an artifact focus largely stems from the distinction between the concepts of ready to hand and present at hand. Recently, Verbeek [20] has proposed that artifacts need not be either ready to hand or present at hand, but can be both at the same time. He illustrates this possibility by considering the difference between a CD player and a piano [20, p. 194]:

Someone who plays the piano is directed toward the music and at the same time is substantially involved with the piano itself. When the same piece is played on a CD player, the artifact that mediates between the person and the music is present in an entirely different way. The machinery of a CD player disappears into the background, withdrawing so that people are only engaged with the music and not with its means of production. A piano, however, is never entirely ready-to-hand, but neither is it exclusively present-at-hand – its machinery is not completely in the background, but not entirely in the foreground either.

In this example, the CD player functions as the perfect assistant, to which the task of playing the music can be completely offloaded. In contrast, the piano requires that the human stays in the loop and operates the piano on a moment-to-moment basis. By proposing that pure readiness to hand is only achieved with complete offloading (i.e., with full automation), Verbeek [20] proposes that pure readiness to hand implies that the human is out of the loop. This proposal fundamentally reconceptualizes readiness to hand by dissociating it from skilled human performance. According to Verbeek [20], skilled human performance instead involves that the artifact is simultaneously ready to hand and present at hand – like a piano or a hammer.

Verbeek [20] also contends that a purely present-to-hand artifact does not necessarily indicate a negatively experienced breakdown in the use of the artifact; it may also indicate that the user is absorbed in cherishing the artifact rather than in using it as a means to an end. This contention accords with many UX studies of users' experiences of the aesthetic and other non-instrumental qualities of their possessions [e.g., 8, 14]. Cherishing may to some extent be about possessing the artifact and, thereby, not fully applicable to artifacts that are operated by the user but owned by the workplace. Yet, a sizable number of people have work tools available in a near permanent manner that approaches ownership.

4   Conclusion

Verbeek's [20] elaboration of the concepts of ready to hand and present at hand offers a way of restructuring and simplifying the insights from the analysis of the four perspectives on how UX may contribute to wellbeing at work, see Table 2. This restructuring leads to three conclusions:

First, when artifacts are present at hand the users focus on the artifact rather than their tasks. While this artifact focus may be associated with positive, artifact-cherishing experiences, it is often triggered by breakdowns in artifact use. To contribute to wellbeing at work, artifacts must be designed so that it is easy to restore their functioning after a breakdown.

Table 2. What may UX contribute to wellbeing at work?

Artifact is…	Focus	UX contribution to wellbeing at work
Present at hand	Artifact	• Breakdown in use (negative UX) • Cherishing the artifact (positive UX)
Both present at hand and ready to hand	Task	• Expressive power, transparency, and possibly structure (positive UX)
Ready to hand	Consumption	• Perceptive and adaptive assistant (positive UX) • Deskilling and monotony (negative UX)

Second, when artifacts are simultaneously present at hand and ready to hand the users are conscious that they are using an artifact but their focus is on their task. Following the tool and media perspectives, artifacts that enable a task focus foster positive UX by lending the users expressive power, by being transparent and, possibly, by structuring the interaction. Importantly, Verbeek's [20] reconceptualization does away with the question of whether positive UX is possible within the tool perspective.

Third, when artifacts are ready to hand they autonomously produce outputs for the users to consume. This consumption focus is experienced positively when the artifact serves the user as a perceptive and adaptive assistant and negatively when the user must abide the system. Thus, the dialogue-partner perspective may foster positive UX through ready-to-hand artifacts, while the system perspective fosters negative UX by leaving the user out of not just the activity loop but also the decision loop.

It should be noted, in closing, that the four perspectives revisited in this study are exclusively about post-design experiences with artifacts. Neither the four perspectives, nor the concepts of ready to hand and present at hand, concern themselves with how artifacts are designed. Yet, user influence on the design of the artifacts employed in performing work tasks may be an additional UX contribution to wellbeing at work [11].

References

1. Braverman, H.: Labor and Monopoly Capital: The Degradation of Work in the Twentieth Century. Monthly Review Press, New York (1974)
2. Chen, P.Y., Cooper, C. (eds.): Wellbeing: A Complete Reference Guide, volume III: Work and wellbeing. Wiley, New York (2014)
3. Colbert, M.: User experience of communication before and during rendezvous: Interim results. Pers. Ubiquit. Comput. **9**(3), 134–141 (2005)
4. Cooper, C.L., Leiter, M.P. (eds.): The Routledge Companion to Wellbeing at Work. Routledge, New York (2017)
5. Fischer, G., Lemke, A.C., Mastaglio, T.: Critics: an emerging approach to knowledge-based human-computer interaction. Int. J. Man Mach. Stud. **35**(5), 695–721 (1991)
6. Fisher, C.D.: Conceptualizing and measuring wellbeing at work. In: Chen, P.Y., Cooper, C.L. (eds.) Wellbeing: A Complete Reference Guide. Volume III: Work and Wellbeing, pp. 9–33. Wiley, New York (2014)
7. Gawande, A.: The upgrade: Why doctors hate their computers. The New Yorker, pp. 62–73 (2018)
8. Hassenzahl, M., Tractinsky, N.: User experience - a research agenda. Behav. Inf. Technol. **25**(2), 91–97 (2006)
9. Heidegger, M.: Being and Time (Macquarrie, J., Robinson, E., Trans.). Harper, New York (1962/1927)
10. Hekkert, P.: Design aesthetics: principles of pleasure in product design. Psychol. Sci. **48**(2), 157–172 (2006)
11. Hertzum, M., Torkilsheyggi, A.: How do users perceive a design-in-use approach to implementation? a healthcare case. In: Lamas, D., Loizides, F., Nacke, L., Petrie, H., Winckler, M., Zaphiris, P. (eds.) INTERACT 2019. LNCS, vol. 11748, pp. 410–430. Springer, Cham (2019). https://doi.org/10.1007/978-3-030-29387-1_23
12. Hornbæk, K., Hertzum, M.: Technology acceptance and user experience: a review of the experiential component in HCI. ACM Trans. Comput.-Hum. Interact. **24**(5), 1–30 (2017). Article 33
13. ISO 9241: Ergonomics of human-system interaction - Part 210: Human-centred design for interactive systems. International Standard Organization, Geneva, CH (2010)
14. Jordan, P.W.: Human factors for pleasure in product use. Appl. Ergon. **29**(1), 25–33 (1998)
15. Kammersgaard, J.: Four different perspectives on human-computer interaction. Int. J. Man Mach. Stud. **28**(4), 343–362 (1988)
16. Lazar, J., Jones, A., Shneiderman, B.: Workplace user frustration with computers: an exploratory investigation of the causes and severity. Behav. Inf. Technol. **25**(3), 239–251 (2006)
17. Meneweger, T., Wurhofer, D., Fuchsberger, V., Tscheligi, M.: Factory workers' ordinary user experiences: an overlooked perspective. Hum. Technol. **14**(2), 209–232 (2018)
18. Roto, V., Law, E., Vermeeren, A., Hoonhout, J.: User experience white paper: Bringing clarity to the concept of user experience. Result from Dagstuhl Seminar (2011). http://www.allaboutux.org/uxwhitepaper. Accessed 1 Apr 2019
19. Trevino, L.K., Lengel, R.H., Daft, R.L.: Media symbolism, media richness, and media choice in organizations: a symbolic interactionist perspective. Commun. Res. **14**(5), 553–574 (1987)
20. Verbeek, P.-P.: What Things Do: Philosophical Reflections on Technology, Agency, and Design. Pennsylvania State University Press, University Park (2005)
21. Winograd, T., Flores, F.: Understanding Computers and Cognition: A New Foundation for Design. Ablex, Norwood (1986)

The "aftermath" of Industry 4.0 in Small and Medium Enterprises

João Silva[1], João Carlos Ferreira[2(✉)], and Frederica Gonçalves[3]

[1] Instituto Universitário de Lisboa (ISCTE-IUL), Lisbon, Portugal
silva.joao.pedro.goncalves@gmail.com
[2] Instituto Universitário de Lisboa (ISCTE-IUL), ISTAR-IUL, Lisbon, Portugal
jcafa@iscte-iul.pt
[3] ITI/Universidade da Madeira, Funchal, Portugal
frederica.goncalves@m-iti.org

Abstract. With the development of new technologies and methodologies, multiple sectors start to experience the benefits and drawbacks. Currently, the industry is facing a new revolution known as Industry 4.0. This new path al-lowed all enterprises to further develop their methodologies and understand the disadvantages and advantages of it. With the sole purpose of retaining costs in production while maintaining the same degree of quality, companies desire to diminish their downtime due to malfunction or improper maintenance schedules that may not amount to the desired efficiency. Nevertheless, not all companies manage to enter this exclusive circle, since such technologies also deliver a high cost which some companies simply cannot support. Consequently, this generates a huge drawback to the outsiders of this revolution.

Keywords: Industry 4.0 · Cyber Physical Systems

1 Introduction

"Companies and their industrial processes need to adapt to this rapid change if they are not to be left behind by developments in their sector and by their competitors." [1]. Industries worldwide are becoming highly volatile, facing the same rhythms as their markets of choice. Taking in consideration the "big step" taken in industry regarding the systems being used, most companies face a problem regarding the data registered in their systems. Although it is collected, proper storage and analysis is not performed resulting in the incapability to extract viable knowledge crucial to decision making [2]. Consequently, this affects multiple areas of action such as maintenance, operations, etc. Therefore, companies must change their mindset to extract vital knowledge. This article aims to analyze the main components that lie within Industry 4.0, advantages of its implementations and understand the main differences between SME's and MNE's. With this research the main goal is to and answer the research question: Is it possible that the main characteristics that define SME's justify the reason why they hold possible investments regarding the methodologies and practices inherent to this revolution?

© IFIP International Federation for Information Processing 2020
Published by Springer Nature Switzerland AG 2020
J. Abdelnour Nocera et al. (Eds.): INTERACT 2019, LNCS 11930, pp. 26–33, 2020.
https://doi.org/10.1007/978-3-030-46540-7_3

2   Industry 4.0

Taking in consideration the developments led on during the past revolutions, a new development was needed to take full capabilities of the current information systems and produce a new output. As known, with the development of information systems in the previous revolution, data started being generated by machines in industries across the world, providing the possibility to create an automated production flow. Nevertheless, data generated was not intended to provide overall view of the production systems, more specifically to the standard maintenance point of view. Since the automation was tackled in this revolution, all the major problems regarding industry were therefore resolved. Nevertheless, the "roads" to increase earnings and productivity were decreasing. Consequently, this led to the new path of Industry 4.0. A path where the main goal was to re-shape previous ideas and concepts, allowing to reproduce models with the current technology available for industry [3].

Throughout time this concept began to grow and became a "revolution" in 2015 propagated by Germany's government as an action to maintain its position as the global leader in the sector of manufacturing equipment. At its core, one cannot state or identify what triggers industry 4.0. "Instead it can be described more precisely by a conjunction of many technologies -both existing and new - which now work together." [4]. Chesworth [5] considers that industry 4.0 is the joint effect of CPS's (Cyber Physical Systems) and IoT (Internet of Things) therefore creating a decentralized control and advanced connectivity. Consequently, large quantities of data are generated justifying the final component of Big Data [5–7]. This joint relation constitutes the key feature of this concept, the smart factory [8].

In terms of benefits to implement the methodologies and components associated with this methodology, follows the table below (Table 1).

Table 1. Advantages of implementing Industry 4.0 [6, 9]

Advantages of implementing Industry 4.0	Sector
Decrease production and logistic costs by 10-30%	Costs
Reduce Quality management costs by 10-20%	Costs
Shorter time-to-market products	Agility/Revenues
Improve customer responsiveness	Customer Experience
Mass production without increasing production costs	Efficiency
Reduce maintenance planning time (20-50%)	Efficiency
Increase equipment uptime (10-20%)	Efficiency
More confidence in data and information	Innovation
Material cost savings (5-10%)	Costs
Reduce inventory carrying costs	Costs
Reduced overall maintenance costs (5-10%)	Costs

The advantages of implementing the practices and methodologies of industry 4.0 trigger interest in all the sectors of industry, yet some already face limitations prior to generating the first step towards this new world.

3   Industry 4.0 Effect in SME

"Small and Medium-sized Enterprises (SME's) are the driving force of many manufacturing economies." [7]. Taking in consideration their position on each country's economy, the impacts of this latest industrial revolution are important to take in consideration. Even though these aren't the only type of enterprises in the world, they face more challenges and limitations than Multi-National Enterprises (MNE's). These two types of companies differ in multiple aspects as literature states. According to the European Commission [10], SME's consist of companies with a staff headcount of 250 or less and turnover that does not exceed 50 million Euros. Nevertheless, further differences arise regarding these two types of companies. Table 2 contains the main differences regarding SME's and MNE's in an overall perspective.

Table 2. Main differences between SME's and MNE's [7]

Feature	SME's	MNE's
(1) Financial Resources	Low	High
(2) Use of advanced Manufacturing	Low	High
(3) Research and Development	Low	High
(4) Human Resources Engagement	Multiple domains	Specific domains
(5) Knowledge and Experience	Focused in a specific area	Spread around different areas
(6) Important activities	Outsourced	Internal
(7) Alliances with Universities	Low	High
(8) Organization culture	Low	High

As stated above, SME's due to their small size, face a tremendous limitation due to their lack of resources, both physical and financial [7]. Nevertheless, exceptions rise in specific areas such aerospace and defense.

Regarding **financial sector (1)**, one of most vital sectors in these companies, a significant disparity lays between the two types of companies. For starters, SME's that want to obtain finance must face expensive process handlings. In other words, the cost of applying for a lone are nothing but immoderate. Legal fees, administrative costs and costs related regarding information related to the acquisition are fixed, regardless of the amount to be loaned. Further costs must be applied in the presence of outside financiers. All these points together with lack of information and proper financial facilities in developing countries leads to a more severe problem.

The low amount of financial resources leads to a chain of consequences, which can be described as a snowball effect for the SME's. In terms of **advanced manufacturing (2),** the usage is considered low, since the investment in advanced manufacturing technologies is difficult to support. This lack of usage leads to incapability to invest in **research and development (3)**. This deeply affects the human resources sector. Instead, the **engagement of human resources (4)** is in multiple domains, "For example, the employees at SME's are more likely to be 'Jack of all Trades' and less likely to develop high levels of expertise." [7]. This leads to the fact that operators in SME's do not manage to gain a proper **specialization in a specific area (5)**, since the responsibilities inherited can range to multiple areas. This type of example does not present in MNE's due to their rich mass of employees. In these types of enterprises, the chances of an employee specialization in a certain area are higher due to sole focus performing related tasks [7].

The consequences of this methodology can easily be applied to production. A low skillset, and engagement lead to the **outsourcing of production (6)** to control costs and time. Due to inability to attain a proper specialization, SME's no longer sustain a proper platform to attract universities and institutes. Consequent to this lack of self-updating policy to maintain up-to-date and cutting-edge methodologies leads to SME's not being able to generate **alliances with universities and institutes (7)**.

With the financial, human resources and production sectors affected by this snowball link, the structure of the company is going to "feel" the consequences. With the outsourcing of production and low skill of collaborators, the **company culture (8)** become poor with low capability to dynamize [7].

These can be stated as the most relevant aspects in a theoretical stand point. Nevertheless, they do not differ from the main studies performed in conducted to SME's. According to the digital business readiness study, "Many enterprises are lacking financial and often human resource too, to promote digital change internally" [5]. This leads a low level of completely digitally up-to-date enterprises of 27%. The main reason behind this low percentage can be explained with the fact that "SME's are lacking confidence in information security and data protection. Without this confidence, the transformation of business and manufacturing processes threatens to stall" [11].

4   Case Study at a Portuguese Company

A Portuguese company with a production lines with heterogeneity of equipment, showed in Fig. 1. From initial analysis and the interview conducted in this company it was inferred that the four machines generate in a total of nine types of log files. Each of these Log files is generated under different circumstances and with different time-spans. In other words, since these are automatically generated and updated in each machine, they must be extracted within a week from its creation to safeguard the data generated. The first data extraction contained data regarding the previous week of operations. To allow the creation of a continuous dataset for analysis, it was established to perform weekly extractions, preferentially at the beginning of the week (Mondays), to streamline the process of communication and data transfer in the project. This methodology could not produce more substantial advantages regarding the SPI machine, since it does not allow for data extraction while machine is in operations. The unscheduled stops in the production lines are registered in loco by the operators, which are then processed and stored in a custom Database (DB), Access Database. Regarding maintenance plans, executions and reports, these are registered in Excel files without being processed and stored in a database. The Central DB can be considered as the bridge between sales, production and logistic departments holding data regarding their daily basis of operations.

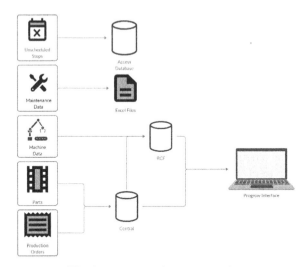

Fig. 1. Data flow of HFA production

Since the files maintained the same structure, any content deviation generated a trigger in the script. Consequently, it led to the entire row of data being sent to quarantine, therefore safeguarding the output file and the database for possible corruption due to unexpected data insertion. The quarantine file would be analysed at the end of the script executions to understand what data was generated incorrectly by the machine.

The process of data integration resembled Extract Transform Load (ETL) methodologies. The reason behind this statement relies on the fact that this methodology allows the system to perform a second analysis of the data regarding its content. In other words, by analysing the data in the output files before inserting in the database it is possible to understand incorrect data type insertion and therefore prevent possible errors. Therefore, quarantine tables were added in the database to hold incorrect values or rows from the files. Once the data is inserted correctly in the database, the last step is to assess the quarantine tables and understand why the rows were redirected.

Once data is stored properly, and a time-frame is generated with enough delta for analysis, the following step is to breakdown the features by understanding which can provide a better result in terms of algorithm predictions. In this step, two datasets are analysed, from the two pick and place machines. The analysis conducted to the files allowed to achieve linkage between the ERR_LOG and LOT_LOG, through the timestamps. This relation further enhanced the dataset by understanding what type of board was being produced in each error registered.

From the original 54 features obtained through the linkage of the two datasets of P&P1 and 2, modifications were executed to discard features that did not uphold vital weight into the prediction stage.. Features such as temperature, vibration and engine metrics were not available, since the types of equipment do not contain sensors to attain such information and engine metrics are not registered.

The second step regards the discard of irrelevant features. The features shown in Table 3 were discarded from both machine's data since they did not register information that could be used for prediction. Also, the feature OPERATOR_CALL_TIME was discarded only in the dataset of P&P2 since it only contains NA values. Further 18 features were discarded in both datasets because they regarded the split of START_DATE_TIME, SETUP_DATE_TIME and FINISH_DATE_TIME. The reason behind this action is due to the fact these features can uphold a viable weight in the Data Visualization stage. With this operation, the number of features available changed from 54 into 27 in P&P1 and 26 in P&P2. From the execution of the algorithms, it was possible to extract the results available in Table which shows the three best datasets and their results in each algorithm for the two P&P machines. Full results are available in annexe N (P&P1) and annexe O (P&P2).

Table 3. Algorithm's results for P&P1 and 2

Machine	Features	Algorithm	Accuracy (%)
Pick and Place 1	D1 TRANSFER_CT_MAX TRANSFER_CT_MIN STANDBY_CT_AVE	NB	20.67
		SVM	44.13
		Adaboost	43.02
	D4 PICK_UP_ERROR PARTS_VISION_ERROR MARK_VISION_ERROR	NB	13.41
		SVM	44.69
		Adaboost	46.93
	D7 OPERATOR_CALL_TIME MARKREC_CT_MAX MARKREC_CT_AVE	NB	07.82
		SVM	49.72
		Adaboost	50.84
Pick and Place 2	D1 WORKING_RATIO MOUNT_RATE MOUNTED_BLOCKS	NB	20.00
		SVM	44.65
		Adaboost	44.65
	D5 TRANSFER_CT_MAX TRANSFER_CT_MIN STANDBY_CT_AVE	NB	26.98
		SVM	40.97
		Adaboost	43.72
	D10 RECOVERY_TIME NO_PARTS_ERROR MOUNT_CT_MAX	NB	35.81
		SVM	41.86
		Adaboost	41.86

Results fluctuate regarding each dataset and model as expected since no sub-dataset is the same. From the initial analysis, it is possible to see that the model with the lowest results overall was NB (lowest result of 8% accuracy and highest of 36%). Regarding the

SVM and Adaboost, the results obtained are similar. More specifically, for the datasets D1 and D10 in P&P2 the two models obtained the same accuracy. Nevertheless, it is possible to see that the best result was obtained through the usage of Adaboost in P&P1 (51% accuracy in D7) and P&P2 (44% accuracy in D1), since also in D5 (P&P2) it obtained a higher accuracy (45%) once compared to SVM. Regarding the overall results, it is possible to see three features that match both pick and place machines (D5 and D1) obtaining average results compared to the remaining ones.

5 Conclusions

From the analysis conducted throughout this paper regarding Industry 4.0 and main features of SME's and MNE's it is possible to understand the main reasons that support the lack of investment in new technologies. Latest achievements regarding methodologies and practices require a solid foundation and finance, to provide a sustainable growth for SME's which justifies the holdback from SME's.

Due to their lack of positioning in current markets, which are more and more competitive, these companies desire fast solutions to their problems, therefore maintaining methodologies that MNE's tested and approved throughout the years. Due to their capability to shape-shift into their desired solution, these companies must face the output of the market in a short-term basis, therefore invalidating the main basis of thought regarding industry 4.0. This line of thought regards a long-term vision where hefty finance is a fixed variable in the equation of going a step towards new income. SME's behave in a solid perspective where they "Don't take a step bigger than their leg". Nonetheless, this strategy to maintain position may provide negative consequences, more considerably inadequate health in a long-term statement, due to their lack of capability to self-innovate and achieve new competitive advantages. Therefore, this confirms the simple line of survival, where the runt of the litter dies.

For SME's to enter this revolution without compromising their structure they must understand the possible implementations that allow to achieve the best results with a low initial investment. This step is vital to stop the snowball effect described in this paper. **One possible solution is the creation of a new framework**. In other words, by providing a "step-by-step" approach, vital information can be attained in a simplified way allowing SME's to understand prior to implementation phase which elements of Industry 4.0 can be implemented and how.

References

1. Finance, C.: Industry 4.0 Challenges and Solutions for Digital Transformation, p. 32 (2015)
2. Efthymiou, K., Papakostas, N.: On a predictive maintenance platform for production systems. Procedia CIRP **3**, 221–226 (2012). https://doi.org/10.1016/J.PROCIR.2012.07.039
3. Meissner, H., Ilsen, R., Aurich, J.C.: Analysis of control architectures in the context of industry 4.0. Procedia CIRP **62**, 165–169 (2017). https://doi.org/10.1016/J.PROCIR.2016.06.113
4. Sakib, N., Wuest, T.: Challenges and opportunities of condition-based predictive maintenance: a review. Procedia CIRP **78**, 267–272 (2018). https://doi.org/10.1016/J.PROCIR.2018.08.318
5. Chesworth, D.: Industry 4.0 Techniques as a Maintenance Strategy (A Review Paper) (2018). https://doi.org/10.13140/rg.2.2.18116.32644

6. Rojko, A.: Industry 4.0 concept: background and overview. Int. J. Inter. Mob. Technol. (iJIM) 11, 77 (2017). https://doi.org/10.3991/ijim.v11i5.7072
7. Mittal, S., Khan, M.A., Romero, D., Wuest, T.: A critical review of smart manufacturing & Industry 4.0 maturity models: Implications for small and medium-sized enterprises (SMEs). J. Manuf. Syst. **49**, 194–214 (2018). https://doi.org/10.1016/J.JMSY.2018.10.005
8. Wang, S., Wan, J., Li, D., Zhang, C.: Implementing smart factory of industrie 4.0: an outlook. Int. J. Distrib. Sens. Netw. **12**, 3159805 (2016). https://doi.org/10.1155/2016/3159805
9. Coleman, C.D., Deuel, S.: Predictive maintenance and the smart factory, p. 8 (2017)
10. What is an SME? | Internal Market, Industry, Entrepreneurship and SMEs, 01 June 2019. https://ec.europa.eu/growth/smes/business-friendly-environment/sme-definition_en
11. Sommer, L.: Industrial revolution - Industry 4.0: are German manufacturing SMEs the first victims of this revolution? J. Ind. Eng. Manag. 8 (2015). https://doi.org/10.3926/jiem.1470

User Persona of Mother of Preterm Neonate

Ganesh Bhutkar[1]([⊠]) [iD], Aditya Dongre[1], Shahaji Deshmukh[2], Lene Nielsen[3] [iD], and Jaydeep Joshi[1]

[1] Centre of Excellence in HCI, Vishwakarma Institute of Technology, Pune, India
ganesh.bhutkar@vit.edu
[2] Bharati Hospital, Bharati Vidyapeeth Deemed University, Pune, India
[3] Business IT Department, IT University of Copenhagen, Copenhagen, Denmark

Abstract. This research paper presents the design process of creating a user persona of Indian mothers of preterm neonates. Many of these preterm neonates require hospitalization in Neonatal Intensive Care Units (NICUs), leading to mental stress for mothers and their families. The main objective of mother's persona is to understand the mother behavior and preferences for designing app for these mothers. The mother's persona is proposed based on hypothesis, user interviews and data analysis. The result shows that the participant mothers of preterm neonates are graduates and homemakers from semi-urban areas around Pune, India. These mothers prefer non-vegetarian diet, they visit a pediatrician more frequently and presently. Moreover, the mothers have challenges with care and anxieties related to their neonates. They do not use any mobile healthcare app or YouTube videos for information about neonatal care. In the future, a mobile app will be developed for these mothers with due consideration to their user persona.

Keywords: User persona · Mother · Preterm neonate · Neonatal ICU · Mother's persona

1 Introduction

India is the second-most populated country in the world, with about 1365 million people [16], including about 653 million women [4]. Its population is growing, recently with a crude birth rate of 18.6 births per thousand population [2]. The effective population growth is about 1.1% per year, adding more than 15 million people to the Indian population [3]. Such high population growth results into national issues like unemployment, increased poverty level, unequal distribution of income, over-strained infrastructure, over-stretched health and educational services [12]. The challenging environment has led to deteriorating health conditions of women inflicting their pregnancies. It also results in too early, too late or too frequent pregnancies, creating complications at the time of childbirth. There is a need to use Information and Communication Technology (ICT) for advising and guiding these mothers on their health condition, along with growth tracking of their neonates, who are infants with an age of upto four weeks.

For usefulness of ICT to women in challenging healthcare conditions, the development process needs to take into account the work conditions of both the clinical staff

© IFIP International Federation for Information Processing 2020
Published by Springer Nature Switzerland AG 2020
J. Abdelnour Nocera et al. (Eds.): INTERACT 2019, LNCS 11930, pp. 34–43, 2020.
https://doi.org/10.1007/978-3-030-46540-7_4

and the mothers. The developers or researchers working with ICT do not have enough exposure to work environments such as Intensive Care Units (ICU). It generates a vital gap in the understanding of mothers of preterm neonates and their hospitalization in Neonatal Intensive Care Units (NICU). Lack of information may include understanding about the mothers' requirements, preferences, day-to-day activities and the stress generated during hospitalization. This paper presents a case that aims at reducing the gap of knowledge through fieldwork in NICU and a proposed mother's persona.

2   Related Work

In this section, we present a few papers that are helpful in the understanding of the work environment in the NICU, the psychology of parents of preterm neonates and the use of personas in health-related ICT. The papers have created a foundation for forming a hypothesis; especially related to the healthcare domain.

In an Italian study, Bouwstra et al. [1] examine the parent-to-neonate bonding experience in NICU. This research paper reveals that the parents of the hospitalized neonate are insecure about whether their neonate responds differently to them than to the medical staff. The mother is always eager to be together with her neonate, especially for breastfeeding and may not be able to meet the neonate frequently throughout the day, which will be depicted in the hypothesis. The Indian research paper by Patil et al. reveals that mothers of a preterm neonate experience significant psychological distress, with elevated anxiety [12]. This study also points out the emotional problems of the mothers and their need for support. Thus, these mothers face an increased mental stress, which will be highlighted in the hypothesis.

A study from the USA, by Heidari et al. [6] states that due to a busy occupational schedule most of the fathers find it challenging to attend all the time to the mothers during hospitalization as well as follow-up hospital visits. Thus, most of the mothers are accompanied by their mothers or relatives. This is similar to our case and will be reflected in the hypothesis. Finally, a study conducted in South Africa by Mburu et al. [7] aims to use technology to support mothers of preterm infants. In this case, the mothers get to know the neonatal status information via text message, over the phone or through digital video. Similarly, Indian mothers get appointment reminders over a phone call or via text message, which is reflected in the hypothesis.

Personas [11] is a popular UX method to understand the involved users. e.g. within healthcare ICT products. As mentioned by van Velsen et al. [13], it has the potential to be a useful tool for designing usable eHealth services. Looking at the field, most personas are related to self-monitoring and tracking such as a public website with cancer-related information [5], a handheld device to monitor chronic heart failure [15] or well-being [14].

3   Field Work

The research has been conducted in two local hospitals located in Pune, India. The larger hospital is housed in huge multi-story buildings with a capacity of more than 500 beds. Multispecialty departments have various units like Emergency, ICU, Burn centre and NICU. Preterm neonates who need intensive medical attention are often admitted into a special area of the hospital called the Neonatal Intensive Care Unit

(NICU). This unit combines advanced technology and trained healthcare professionals to provide specialized care for the tiniest patients as seen in Fig. 1. It has continuing care areas for neonates who have health issues and need skilled nursing care. Such NICUs are categorized in different levels [8]. NICU at Level I, looks after neonates who need more care than healthy neonates and require regular monitoring assistance. NICU at Level II provides special care where nurses are assigned to 3-4 neonates for constant attention and care. NICU at Level III take care of very sick neonates providing prolonged lung ventilation-support. **A neonatologist typically leads NICU and staffed with intensivists, nurses, therapists and dietitians.** Neonatologists are pediatricians with additional training in the care of sick and preterm neonates [8, 9].

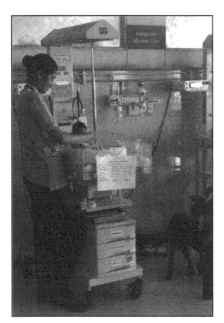

Fig. 1. A typical work environment in Neonatal ICU (NICU)

The research in NICU has started with the design of hypothesis about mothers of preterm neonates mainly focused on their personal traits, the medical context and mobile usage in practice. A questionnaire, designed on the basis of the hypothesis, has been used for interviews of selected mothers. To facilitate the active participation of mothers, the questions for the interviews are also provided in the local regional language - Marathi along with English. The field work started with interviews of physicians and nurses working with NICUs while forming the hypothesis. The main participants of these interviews have been 19 mothers of preterm neonates. Initially, about 15 mothers of preterm neonates have been interviewed and for further clarifications on related doubts, the interviews of 4 more mothers have been conducted. In all these interviews, the aim has been to get the details about demographic information, sources of information for mothers, their preferences, related facts, challenges and issues in the work environment of NICUs. The participating mothers of preterm neonates have been in the age group of

18–32 years. Most of these mothers are graduates from semi-urban areas around Pune. They were married between the age of 18 to 25 years and are housewives/home-makers. Most neonates are their first child.

The interviews have been conducted three days over a fortnight. Each interview lasted for 15–20 min. The research team had limited medical knowledge despite putting sufficient effort into an understanding of the neonatal context. **The all-male team in Pune has faced difficulties during the initial interviewing process of mothers due to gender incompatibility and therefore, a female intern from one of the hospitals is included as an interviewer of the mothers.** This intern has been there to help in sharing expectations, priorities and experiences of these mothers.

4 Construction of Proposed User Persona

In this qualitative research, the user is the mother of a preterm neonate. A related user persona of a mother is proposed to analyze the maternal experience in NICUs. This study aims to understand a typical Indian mother, her experience and challenges in NICU. The process of creating the neonate mother personas started with formation of a hypothesis [10]. **The hypothesis is mainly focused on their personality, medical traits and active mobile usage.** The assumptions include demographic information such as age, education, marriage age, area, occupation and others as depicted in Fig. 2. The health and medical science traits include - personal Body Mass Index (BMI), diet, medication schedule, knowledge of medical terms/equipment, mental/physical stress and others. The mobile usage section includes factors such as internet access, use of messenger app, local language support, m-Health app usage, social media groups and so on. Based on all these factors, the hypothesis of mother of preterm neonate is created with more than 30 statements.

Topic: User Persona of Mother of Preterm Neonate

Hypothesis for Mother of Preterm Neonate

[A] Mother's Personality:

1. Mother belongs to the age group of 18-25 years.
2. She has completed her education till 12th Std.
3. She got married at 18 years or more of her age.
4. She stays in or belongs to rural area.
5. She is a housewife / homemaker.
6. She travels at least 3-5 KM daily using public transport.

[B] Health / Medical Science:

1. She has BMI less than 18.5 or more than 25.
2. She has delivered a preterm neonate within 18 months of her marriage.
3. She has delivered a preterm neonate as a first neonate.
4. Her preterm neonate is delivered before 37 weeks.
5. She is hospitalized for a longer duration along with her neonate than that of mothers with normal deliveries.

Fig. 2. A section of hypothesis of mother of preterm neonate

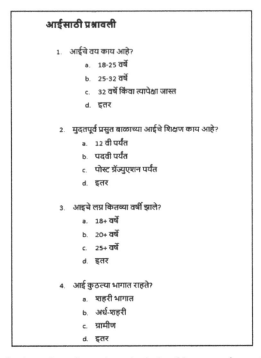

Fig. 3. A section of questionnaire in local language for mothers

After proposing the hypothesis, a questionnaire has been prepared for conduction of interviews of selected mothers in hospitals, during the field work. A questionnaire seen in Fig. 3, is in Marathi, the local language to facilitate active participation of mothers in the interviews. It has more than 30 objective questions with upto 4 options. More than one-third questions are of YES/NO type. Using this questionnaire, interviews of mothers of preterm neonates have been conducted in NICUs. The interviews of main participant mothers have been conducted to get the details about demographic information, sources of information for mothers, their preferences, related facts, challenges and issues in work environment of NICUs. The more details of interviews and data collection process are elaborated in the section about Field Work.

The collected interview data has been analyzed to get vital findings/insights, capturing mother's experience in NICU. The related detailed user persona and interesting observations made on the basis of hypothesis are presented in the next section – The Mother Persona.

5   The Mother Persona

The results of interviews mainly consist of accepted and rejected statements in proposed hypothesis as well as the user persona of mother of preterm neonate. Participant mothers of preterm neonates have been mainly in the age group of 18–32 years. Most of these mothers are graduates from semi-urban areas around Pune, India. Most of them were married within 18 to 25 years range and are housewives/homemakers, as depicted in a graph on mother's occupation in Fig. 4. Most of the mothers prefer non-vegetarian diet and visit more frequently a pediatrician than gynecologist, as seen in a graph related with visits to physicians in Fig. 5.

Most neonates are their first child and spontaneous preterm infants. These mothers are always eager to be with their neonates especially for breast-feeding, but are not able to meet the neonates frequently; especially during nights. Most of them do not use any m-Health app, as seen in a Fig. 6. They do not join any user group related with neonate/pregnancy care on social media, but read related blogs. These mothers communicate with physician in person and also, take appointments in person or over a phone.

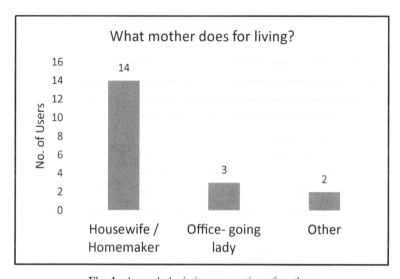

Fig. 4. A graph depicting occupation of mothers

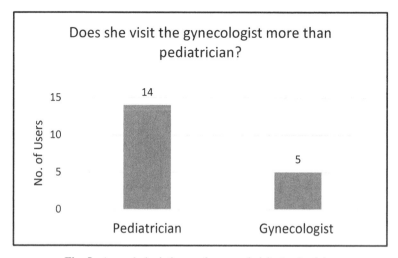

Fig. 5. A graph depicting preference of visits to physician

Most of them do not use YouTube videos for information about neonate/pregnancy care, as seen in Fig. 7.

Figure 8 depicts the user persona of mother of preterm neonate and is proposed based on accepted/corrected statements in proposed hypothesis. This mother persona depicts the details about demographic information, sources of information for mothers, their preferences, related facts, challenges and issues in the work environment of NICUs.

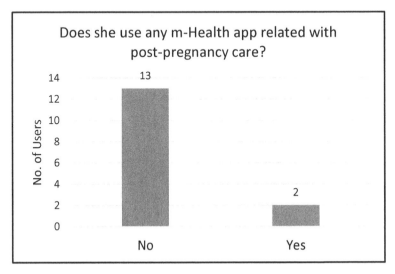

Fig. 6. A graph depicting usage of m-Health apps

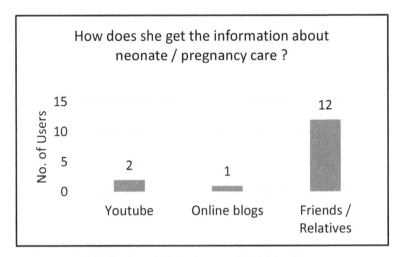

Fig. 7. A graph depicting use of YouTube videos

MOTHER'S PERSONA

RESEARCH GOAL

To study the user experience of Mothers of Neonates during hospitalization

DEMOGRAPHIC INFORMATION

LOCATION: **Pune, INDIA (Semi-Urban)**
AGE: **25+ Years**
GENDER: **Female**
OCCUPATION: **Homemaker**
EDUCATION LEVEL: **Graduate**
Age of Marriage: **21+ Years**
Diet: **Non-veg**
BMI Deviation: **(BMI < 18 & 25 < BMI)**

SOURCES OF INFORMATION

- Counseling by Physicians
- Interactions with Nurses
- Messengers & Online Blogs
- Mother, Relatives & Friends

CHALLENGES & ISSUES

- Fear of neonatal death
- Unfamiliar environment
- Mental and physical stress
- Child safety & security
- Breastfeeding every 3 hours
- Maintaining the BMI
- Hard to maintain infant bonding
- High blood pressure
- Unknown medical terms
- Not exposed to m-Heath app

PREFERENCES & FACTS

- More visits to pediatrician than gynecologist
- Communicates with physician in person
- Does not use YouTube to get awareness regarding pregnancy / infant care
- Does not use even a single m-Health app
- Does not order medicines through mobile app

PERSONA SUMMARY

Demographic Information: Graduate, Homemaker & Deviated BMI
Sources of Information: Counseling by physicians & Interaction with mother
Challenges & Issues: Unfamiliar environment & Mental / physical stress
Preferences & Facts: More visits to pediatrician & No exposure to m-Health apps

Fig. 8. User persona of mother of preterm neonate

6 Conclusion and Future Work

In this paper, a user persona for Mother of Preterm Neonate has been proposed. This user persona has provided interesting insights into demographic information, sources of information for mothers, their preferences, related facts, challenges and issues in the work environment of NICUs. It will help application developers and usability professionals in the design of related healthcare applications. In the future, an Android app will be developed for the mothers of preterm neonates with due consideration to their user persona derived during this research work. Furthermore, how the app fits into the work of the healthcare staff in neonatal care, can also be addressed.

Acknowledgement. We thank the physicians, nursing staff and medical administrators at local hospitals in Pune, India for their cooperation and support during the field work. We appreciate the active participation of medical intern - **Ms. Sheen Bhat** for her enthusiasm and assistance during the interview sessions of mothers of preterm neonates in NICUs. We thank **India Alliance and The African Academy of Sciences (AAS)** for providing **Africa-India Mobility Fund (AIMF) Grant** and supporting ICT research work related with Mothers of Preterm Infants.

References

1. Bouwstra, S., Chen, W., Feijs, L., Oetomo, S., Linden, W., Iisselsteijn, W.: Designing the parents-to-infant bonding experience in the NICU. In: First International Conference on Global Health Challenges, Oct. 2012, Venice, Italy, pp. 7–13 (2012)
2. Crude Birth Rate Statistics by World Data Atlas. https://knoema.com/atlas/India/topics/Demographics/Population-forecast/Crude-birth-rate. Accessed 10 Apr 2019
3. Effective Population Growth. http://worldpopulationreview.com/countries/india-population/. Accessed 23 Apr 2019
4. Female Population in India. http://www.indiaonlinepages.com/population/india-current-population.html. Accessed 24 Apr 2019
5. Goldberg, L., et al.: Usability and accessibility in consumer health informatics. Am. J. Prev. Med. **40**(5), S187–S197 (2011)
6. Heidari, H., Hasanpour, M., Fooladi, M.: The Iranian parents of premature infants in NICU experience stigma of shame. Med. Arh. **66**(1), 35–40 (2012)
7. Mburu, W., Wardle, C., Joolay, Y., Densmore, M.: Co-designing with mother and neonatal unit staff: use of technology to support mothers of preterm infants. In: The 2nd African Conference for Human-Computer Interaction – AfriCHI 2018, Windhoek, Namibia (2018)
8. Neonatal Intensive Care Unit (Wikipedia). https://en.wikipedia.org/wiki/Neonatal_intensive_care_unit. Accessed 26 Apr 2019
9. Neonatal Intensive Care Unit. https://www.stanfordchildrens.org/en/topic/default?id = the-neonatal-intensive-care-unit-nicu-90-P02389. Accessed 22 Apr 2019
10. Nielsen, L.: 10 Steps to Personas. http://personas.dk/?pageid=196. Accessed 26 Apr 2019
11. Nielsen, L.: Personas. User Focused Design. Springer, Heidelberg (2019). https://doi.org/10.1007/978-1-4471-4084-9
12. Patil, A., et al.: Prototype design of android app for mother of preterm infant. In: Barricelli, B., et al. (eds.) HWID 2018. IFIP AIC, vol. 544, pp. 3–16. Springer, Cham (2019). https://doi.org/10.1007/978-3-030-05297-3_1

13. van Velsen, L., van Gemert-Pijnen, L., Nijland, N., Beaujean, D., van Steenbergene J.: Personas: the linking pin in holistic design for eHealth. In: The Fourth International Conference on eHealth, Telemedicine, and Social Medicine - eTELEMED 2012, Valencia, Spain (2012)
14. Vicini, S., Gariglio, A., Alberti, F., Oleari, E., Sanna, A.: Enhancing personas for well-being e-services and product service systems. In: Marcus, A. (ed.) DUXU 2016. LNCS, vol. 9746, pp. 365–376. Springer, Cham (2016). https://doi.org/10.1007/978-3-319-40409-7_35
15. Villalba, E., Peinado I., Arredondo, M.: User interaction design for a wearable and IT-based heart failure system. In: 12th International Conference on Human-Computer Interaction, Beijing, China, pp. 1230–1239 (2007)
16. World Human Population. https://www.worldometers.info/world-population/india-population/. Accessed 10 Apr 2019

Livability- Analysis of People's Living Comfort in Different Cities of India Using GIS: A Prototype

Shrikant Salve[✉], Shubham Bombarde, Ankit Agrawal, Smruti Paldiwal, Bishal Sharma Roy, and Bhagyashree Alhat

MIT Academy of Engineering, Pune, India
shrikantsalve@gmail.com, shubhambombarde4@gmail.com,
ankit.agrawal3097@gmail.com

Abstract. The comfort of living for an average individual plays a crucial factor in urban development. It validates a city's ability to provide all the necessary comfort for modern livability standards. To analyze city livability, in this position paper we have proposed a system that provides a lifestyle overview through locality Indexing of a particular geographical area according to the ease of living for four particular age groups like a child, middle-aged, senior adult, and senior citizen. The system accounts for various indicators like health, transport, population, climate, pollution, crowd, etc. to yield a personalized result. The system consists of a web interface and a python backend which pulls desired data about the location from sources like Google Maps (Places API) and data.gov.in. (Indian Govt. website). This data is then mined and useful/relevant information is summarized to yield an end result. Parallel computations consisting of pattern discovery (by mining algorithms) and data aggregation are carried on a cloud service maintaining a local data store for processed queries. The generated end result is then presented to the user in the form of visualization charts.

Keywords: Livability · GIS · Locality indexing and analysis · Indicators

1 Introduction

Cities are emerging as the prime engines of the Indian economy. They are emerging as the generators of national wealth. India can be looked up to as one among the rapidly urbanizing nations in the world. According to the census report of 2017, India's urban population is 31.16% and there are 46 metropolitan cities [1]. It is necessary for the nation to invest in the social and economic functions of cities. As cities trace the path of Gross Domestic Product (GDP) growth rates by policies which adhere to the quality life, their comfort of living is highly challenged. Providing the person wanting to move to any city along with the complete knowledge of the surrounding of workplace, with least efforts is the main motivation of our project. Therefore, adapting the suitable job location (workplace) supports the person well-being [2].

The locality indexing or livability indexing is the sum of the factors that add up to a community's quality of life-including the built and natural environments, economic prosperity, social stability and equity, educational opportunity, cultural, entertainment and

J. Abdelnour Nocera et al. (Eds.): INTERACT 2019, LNCS 11930, pp. 44–51, 2020.
https://doi.org/10.1007/978-3-030-46540-7_5

recreation possibilities [3]. There can be various types or categories of indexing like physical and natural amenities. It largely depends on the class of the user who is assessing the locality. For example, some people need things to feel safe and secure. The rest might need good schools, transportation, hospitals and so on. Keeping this in mind, livability can be classified into different age groups, to provide a reliable result. Our system provides a lookout into the quality of life in a particular area or region or city as it accounts all the social, economic, environmental and civic factors that determine the possibility of a citizen to live in a city [4]. To get an in-depth idea of this project we have gone through several existing works, that consists of all the possible survey knowledge using Structural Equation Modelling (SEM) and Geographic Information System (GIS) approach.

2   City Livability Index and GIS

Livability encompasses broad human needs ranging from food and basic security to beauty, cultural expression, and a sense of belonging to a community or a place [3]. Nowadays, 31.16% of India lives in an urban area like towns and cities [5]. It is estimated that in the coming 20 years, nearly half of India would be shifting towards urbanized areas [5]. As a result, developing new cities for migration would be a major challenge. The City Livability Index 2010 [3] is a Government of India report which comments on the quality of life that our cities offer. It relies on entirely objective analysis, employing more than 300 indicators on a 10-year timeline series. For evaluating neighborhoods of Nigeria, a Structural Equation Modelling (SEM) approach has been introduced by Iyanda et al. [6]. This study employed a Delphi survey technique on fifteen livable human community experts in South Arica from which the conceptual variables for neighborhood features were developed for the study. A questionnaire survey was conducted among the residents of the selected low-income housing in South Africa. The data collected for the study were analyzed for factorial validity through SEM. The result obtained from the SEM analysis confirms only five indicators out of twenty-two indicators identified from the interview and literature review for the study. This study adopts structural equation modelling (a second order factor) to investigate the key factors of analyzing livability of planned residential neighborhoods in Minna, Nigeria. Using Geographic Information System (GIS) application tools, users can create interactive queries, information analysis, map data edition and display the results [7]. Therefore, we have used GIS to identify the livability index of a particular area.

3   Methodology

According to our survey, we have selected indicators that will fetch datasets corresponding to each of the indicators from sources like Google Places API [8], data.gov.in [9] and kaggle.com [10] into our environment and start standardizing it. Each of the datasets undergoes standardization and indexing in parallel until a raw figure that exhibits a particular indicator is obtained. These raw figures are then saved as variables which are reflected on the results page.

3.1   Identifying Indicators

During literature study from papers, government of India reports, we have identified several indicators are listed in Table 1 below. Livability is defined by a set of factors or

Table 1. Livability indicators

Features	Child (0-15)	MiddleAged (15-30)	SeniorAdult (30-50)	SeniorCitizen (>50)
Population	3	2	0	1
Migration	3	0	1	2
Education	1	0	2	3
Occupation	3	1	0	2
Health & Medical Standards	1	2	3	0
Health Parameter	1	3	2	0
Safety	2	0	1	3
Crime	3	2	0	1
Cyber Crime	2	0	1	3
Road Accidents	2	0	1	3
Housing Options	3	2	0	1
HousingCost & Availability	3	1	0	2
Urban House hold crowding	3	0	1	2
Socio Cultural Env	2	0	1	3
Political Env.	3	2	1	0
Infrastructure	2	0	1	3
Economic Env.	2	0	1	3
Income and employment	3	1	0	2
Economic Infrastructure	3	2	0	1
Business Env.	3	1	0	2
Purchasing Power	3	1	0	2
Planned Env. /City	3	2	0	1
Communication	3	0	1	2
Transportation Infrastructure	2	0	1	3
Labor Participation Rate	2	0	1	2
Open Space Index	2	3	1	0
Energy Index	2	0	1	2
Pollution	2	3	1	0
Climate	1	3	2	0
Food Quality	1	3	2	0
Food Variability	2	1	0	3
Food Availability	0	0	0	0
Water Availability	2	1	0	2
Water	3	2	1	0
Mobility Index	1	0	0	2
Night Life	3	0	1	2
Parking Facility	3	1	0	2
Availability of Public Transport	2	0	3	1
Traffic	3	0	1	2
Handicap Friendliness	3	2	1	0
Tourism Attraction	3	1	0	2

in this paper we called it as 'indicators.' Some of these indicators may carry varying significance for different age groups, which could be ranked among to yield personalized result. Table 2 shows how indicators are grouped and mapped accordingly in specific livability classes, where each class may/may not have some importance over the other. These grouped indicators aim to perfectly imply and achieve all the quality standards essential for current day assessment. Indicators are prioritized among four classes- Child, Middle Aged, Senior Adult, and Senior Citizen depicted in Table 2 [3].

Table 2. Reference Table for Table 1

Level	Importance
0	Highest
1	High
2	Low
3	Lowest

3.2 Fetching Datasets for Indicators

After identification of indicators, the Google Places API, data.gov.in and kaggle.com have used the fetch the dataset for a particular location.

3.3 Indexing Technique

There are different indexing methods [11] explained below. Data is indexed by calculating the following interpretations confined in the spectrum of data points as defined by the dataset.

Dimensional Index Methodology. This method normalizes all the data points within a fixed range (0, 1). This enables to sort and compare any given data points.

$$I = \frac{I(x) - I(\min)}{I(\max) - I(min)} \tag{1}$$

OR

$$I = 1 - \frac{I(x) - I(\min)}{I(\max) - I(min)} \tag{2}$$

For example: Open spaces (Indicator) – Max: 50%, Min: 5% Example of a Pune city where Open Space is 30%: (30-5)/(50-5) = 25/45 = 0.55 is Dimensional Index Methodology.

Z-Score or Standardization. This method classifies the datapoints across the median which helps in interpreting whether a given point has a positive/negative impact depicted in Table 3.

$$I = \frac{x - \mu}{\sigma} \tag{3}$$

Where,

$$\mu = \frac{1}{n} \sum_{n=1}^{\infty} x \, (mean) \tag{4}$$

$$\sigma = \sqrt{\frac{1}{n} \sum_{n=1}^{\infty} (x - \mu)^2} \tag{5}$$

(Standard Deviation)

Table 3. Z-score table

Z Score	Conclusion
Negative	Bad impact of that particular observation
Zero	No/Average impact of that particular observation
Positive	The good impact of that particular observation

Decile Scale Ranking. This method aggregately ranks all the datapoints using a calculated Decile Scale as shown below (Fig. 1).

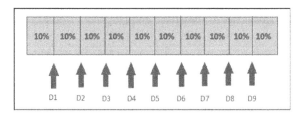

Fig. 1. Decile scale calculation

D(n) = PERCENTILE (data_values[], n/10), where n = [1, 9], data values = array of values.

In the end, we can calculate the ranking of each state based on the values of the decile scale. Similarly, we can compute the rankings for all the indicators taken into account and rank the cities accordingly [11]. The computed decile scale show in Table 4 below. Table 5 depicts the sample indexing method for an indicator. The sample indicators like Health Parameter, Safety, Crime etc. with their respective sample values (taken from datasets like Google Places API, data.gov.in and kaggle.com) taken for reference and their respective Dimensional Index Methodology, Z-score, Decile values were calculated as shown in the Tables 5 and 6.

Table 4. Decile scale

D1	D2	D3	D4	D5	D6	D7	D8	D9
63.89	65.98	68.05	70.12	72.19	75.43	78.66	83.02	88.51

Table 5. Example- sample indexing of an indicator

Sample indicator	Sample values	Dimensional index methodology	Z Score	Decile
Health parameter	67.02	0.162	−0.638	9
Safety	61.80	0.000	−1.053	10
Crime	72.19	0.323	−0.228	6
Cyber crime	94.00	1.000	1.504	1
Road accidents	80.28	0.574	0.415	2

Table 6. Relevant statistics

MAX	94.0
MIN	61.8
MEAN	75.1
STDEV	12.6

The above methods are used to calculate the livability index for different cities, which are also incorporated in the tool that we have proposed for livability analysis. The screen-shot of prototype designed is depicted below.

The screenshot of user interface of developed prototype for livability analysis is depicted in Fig. 2. This tool accepts the name of the place from the user and livability class as input. It displays the livability index of that particular place and also demonstrates each indicator rating in bar-chart format. In Fig. 3, upper right corner displays the livability index of *Jaipur* City and the bar-chart represents the indicators ratings. Below the bar-chart the relevant statistics like Population, Amenities, Climate etc. are displayed. The quick highlights of important factors of city livability.

Livability Analysis

Google Autocomplete   Jaipur, Rajasthan, India

Select Livability Class

Middle Aged   Senior Adult   Senior Citizen
(15-30)   (30-50)   (>50)

Analyse

Fig. 2. The screen-shot-1 of tool's User Interface for Livability Analysis

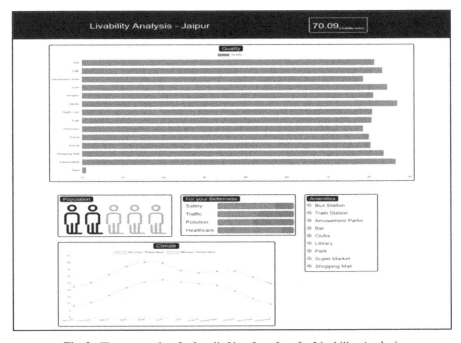

Fig. 3. The screen-shot-2 of tool's User Interface for Livability Analysis

4 Conclusion and Future Scope

The present work is inspired by a web portal 'AARP Livability Index' [12], aiming to incorporate analysis for Indian regions. We have developed a tool (prototype) for calculating the livability index of Indian cities. Livability index support to find out users well-being for particular workplace or city. We work with different data sources to provide a similar, and a bit more enhanced experience that the existing solution by customizing the results based on the user-intended age group. A combined system that can fetch geographical data from sources and process it accordingly for the end-user to deliver a content-rich visualization is henceforth developed. We plan to refine the feature selection and classification process by using machine learning techniques to reduce complexity and to improve the exactness. This project has the potential to evolve as a platform for city surveying and highlighting improvable sectors, which could stand useful for development planning at further stages. Lastly, we intend to make this application accessible to a broad group of end users by hosting it on a cloud service in the near future.

References

1. Urban population (% of data). data.worldbank.org. Accessed 20 Apr 2019
2. Tu, X., Huang, G., Wu, J.: Review of the relationship between urban green space accessibility and human well-being. Shengtai Xuebao/Acta Ecologica Sinica **39**(2), 421–431 (2019). https://doi.org/10.5846/stxb201802030294
3. Confederation of Indian Industry, Liveability index 2010: The best cities in India. A CII: Institute for Competitiveness Report, Northern Region, India (2010). http://indiaenvironmentportal.org.in/files/Liveability-Report.pdf
4. Yin, L., Yin, Y.: Research on assessment of city livability based on principle component analysis-taking shandong province for example. In: International Conference on Management and Service Science 2009, pp. 1–4. IEEE (2009)
5. India Population (2019). https://www.worldometers.info/world-population/india-population/. Accessed 04 Apr 2019
6. Iyanda, S.A., Ismail, O., Fabunmi, F.O., Adeogun, A.S., Mohit, M.A.: Evaluating neighborhoods livability in nigeria: a structural equation modelling (SEM) approach. 5.1. Int. J. Built Environ. Sustain. **5**, 47–55 (2018)
7. Naik, G.M., Aditya, M., Naik, S.B.: GIS-based 4D model development for planning and scheduling of a construction project. Int. J. Innov. Manage. Technol. **2**(6), 447 (2011)
8. Google Maps Places API. https://www.cloud.google.com/maps-platform/places&#x200E. Accessed 4 May 2019
9. Government of India data. https://data.gov.in. Accessed 15 Apr 2019
10. https://www.kaggle.com. Accessed 15 Apr 2019
11. Methodology for collection and computation of livability standards in cities, Ministry of Urban Development, Government of India. http://smartcities.gov.in/upload/uploadfiles/files/MethodologicalReportFinal.pdf
12. AARP Livability Index Homepage. https://livabilityindex.aarp.org/. Accessed 04 Apr 2019

Digital Peer-Tutoring: Early Results from a Field Evaluation of a UX at Work Learning Format in SMEs

Torkil Clemmensen[(✉)] and Jacob Nørbjerg

Copenhagen Business School, Frederiksberg, Denmark
{tc.digi,jno.digi}@cbs.dk

Abstract. Digital Peer-Tutoring is a new learning format that enables production workers in Small to Medium Sized Enterprises (SMEs) to co-design their inter-action with assistive technologies such as collaborative robots. The video-based learning format is based on design thinking and helps shop floor workers create and document solutions to robot interaction problems, and share their how-to knowledge with their colleagues. Early field evaluation results indicated that workers benefit from the Digital Peer-tutoring learning format and produced how-to videos for their colleagues. Furthermore, the Digital Peer-tutoring learning format was also found useful by the company management and ownership as means of documentation and customer communication. Thus, the learning format can also support SMEs on their path to digitalization.

Keywords: Collaborative robots · Assistive technologies · UX at work

1 Introduction

In this paper we propose a new learning format 'Digital Peer-tutoring' as a means to design and share solutions to worker-technology interaction problems in small to medium sized enterprises[1] (SMEs).

Peer tutoring has long been suggested as a way to help students deal with design problems [13]. Design, understood here as design thinking [4], is an iterative process consisting of generative and evaluative stages, which eventually converge on a solution to the design problem. Design thinking is typically applied to solve non-routine, wicked problems in an organization, when there is a need for novel how-to knowledge. To engage in creation and sharing of new how-to knowledge requires hands-on experience, which is where peer tutoring becomes very helpful. The new learning format Digital Peer-Tutoring aims to help workers interacting with collaborative robots on the shop floor to use digital media to engage in teaching and learning with colleagues about their

---

[1] The category of micro, small and medium-sized enterprises (SMEs) consists of enterprises which employ fewer than 250 persons with an annual turnover not exceeding 50 million euro, and/or an annual balance sheet total not exceeding 43 million euro.

© IFIP International Federation for Information Processing 2020
Published by Springer Nature Switzerland AG 2020
J. Abdelnour Nocera et al. (Eds.): INTERACT 2019, LNCS 11930, pp. 52–58, 2020.
https://doi.org/10.1007/978-3-030-46540-7_6

user experiences. We ask the questions: *Can a Digital Peer-Tutoring learning format enable shop floor workers to design positive UXs for themselves and their colleagues? What kind of ethical stance is implied by the use of Digital Peer-Tutoring?*

The paper reports from the initial part of a research project aiming to develop a Digital Peer-Tutoring learning format for shop floor workers in SMEs. The project aims to develop capabilities among shop floor workers to design and document, with short videos, solutions to operational and collaboration issues related to collaborative robots.

The research is situated within the KomDigital regional development project that brings together 18 of the Copenhagen Capital Region's companies, unions, employer associations, and educational institutions. The project aims to improve digital competencies in a broad sense among the employers and employees in SMEs thereby enabling the companies to adopt and implement digital technologies. The target companies come from all sectors, including construction and building, small scale production, product development, and finance, and the technologies include data mining and analysis, collaborative robots and other forms of production automation, AI based financial advice, and more.

KomDigital achieves its goals through new digital learning formats, which can be made available to target companies and organizations. The formats are tailored to the working conditions and needs of companies and employees, so that both employees, managers, companies and organizations can use new digital technologies to expand and grow.

2   Related Work

2.1   Digitalization in SMEs

SMEs depend on their workers' knowledge and innovative capabilities to create new ways of working with technology, and they generally lack the capability and capacity for comprehensive digital transformation [6, 9]. Collaborative robots that work alongside a human worker can be integrated into the production without radical reconfiguration or automation of established workflows. A human worker can program a collaborative robot to perform tasks such as lift, pick and place, move, or otherwise process physical objects [5, 12, 14]. Thus, worker designed interaction with collaborative robots and other assistive technologies is a useful first step towards digitalization in an SME.

2.2   Peer Tutoring

Peer tutoring [7, 13] overlaps somewhat with other notions of providing informal technical help between colleagues, such as over-the-shoulder-learning [17], over-the-shoulder-guidance in tertiary education [2], peer-assisted learning [8] and peer teaching [15] in the medical domain, and over-the-shoulder appropriation [1] and peer interaction [10] in software development.

In this paper we build primarily on the approach put forward by Twidale [17] in that we aim to support the provision of informal technical help between colleagues. Similar to Schleyer et al. [13] we acknowledge the role of peer tutors at various levels towards developing problem solving skills among colleagues. Specifically, we introduce a new role of digital competence facilitator, a 'Digital Coach', as explained below.

2.3 Digital Peer-Tutoring

What distinguishes 'digital peer-tutoring' from traditional peer-tutoring is that the concept builds entirely on the use of video. The idea is that workers learn from creating and redesigning videos while sketching [11] as part of applying design thinking to design their own and their colleagues' work flow and interactions with collaborative robots. Ørngreen et al. [11] suggested to link sketching techniques and creative reflection processes to video productions, and we extent this proposal to cover linking all parts of design thinking (problem definition and user needs finding, sketching, prototyping hypotheses, evaluation) to workers' video production. Secondly, we propose that video-based reasoning, instead of paper or verbal exchange, empower workers to explore and take ownership of their work. Vistisen et al. [18] proposed to support ethical userstances during the design process of products and services, and proposes using animation-based sketching as a design method. We follow that line of thought, though we are less interested in professional designers, and more interested in workers' own production (and consumption) of videos-as-digital-peer-tutoring.

3 Case Setting: A Collaborative Robot in Specialized Glass Manufacturing

After learning from initial talks with three different SMEs in Denmark, we agreed with the ABC company to adapt and evaluate the digital peer-tutoring learning format in one of their production facilities. The ABC company is a European SME specializing in glass processing. The company produces individual pieces and small batches with special specifications as well as entire series of several thousand units.

About a year prior to our visit, the ABC company purchased and installed a 100,000€ collaborative robot in order to explore if and how it could be used in their production. At the time of our visit, the robot was used only during the final polishing steps of one large scale order, and it was idle much of the time. Workers and management agreed, however, that the robot could be used for other purposes as well, and thus enable the company to accept more large batch orders, but no initiatives had been implemented for several months due to lack of time to experiment with the robot. Furthermore, the initial design decision had been a stationary installation, that is, the robot could not be moved to other positions on the floor where it could interact with other machines or workers.

The initial design decisions seemed to be related to a limited initial understanding of the robot's capability and a lack of strategic intent. In any case, it was clear that there was an unexplored potential (and risks) for enhancing the factory's capacity while empowering workers and help them design their own user experiences with the robot.

4 Method: Action Design Research with SMEs

Our approach to building new digital competences in SMEs is inspired by action design research (ADR). ADR argues that IT artifacts are 'ensembles' formed by the organizational context during development and use. Research in this tradition interweaves constructing the IT artifact, intervention in the organization, and evaluating outcomes [16].

We visited the company 6 times over a six-week period during the spring 2019. The purpose of our first visit was to develop insights into the company, the motivation for purchasing the robot, and challenges with its current as well as potential future use of the robot. We observed the robot's current (very limited) use, interviewed and discussed with robot vendors, managers and shop-floor workers, and observed work and demonstrations of the robot.

The digital peer-tutoring learning format (see Sect. 5) was implemented in four sessions over the next four visits, followed by a final evaluation on the sixth visit. We documented all observations, interviews, and learning sessions with video and audio recordings and photos, and we collected the videos produced by the workers.

The learning format was evaluated after each session and at a final one-day meeting with participation from all key stakeholders.

5 The Digital Peer-Tutoring Learning Format

Table 1. Overview of training sessions.

Sessions	Themes	Topics	Worker-created-how-to-videos
1	The problem	Personas Interaction Collaboration with tech.	1. A persona 2. An interaction problem 3. A collaboration problem
2	Solution sketch	How to sketch a solution Interaction Collaboration	Three design ideas for 4. Interaction 5. Collaboration
3	Design prototype	Interaction and collaboration prototypes	6. Elaborate one design idea into a prototype
4	Evaluate prototype	How to evaluate/test prototypes	7. Test the prototype with a colleague

The digital peer-tutoring learning format consisted of an ensemble of instruction-videos, quizzes, example-solution-video, and worker-created-how-to-videos. Together with the case company production site, we designed and implemented four training sessions with selected shop-floor workers (Table 1).

We developed short (3–5 min) instruction videos for each session that explained the theme, introduced techniques that the participants could use to investigate problems and describe solutions, and concluded with an exercise where the participants should develop a short video (3–5 min). We also produced short example videos with our 'answers' to the video assignment for each session.

All video material – including instruction material was recorded with standard smartphone hardware and software, and published without editing, in order to promote a 'simple-yet'sufficient' attitude towards to video production.

For each session, a 'digital competence facilitator' (student assistant) travelled to the factory and discussed the material with the participants, and helped them produce their own 'employee-videos', which were subsequently uploaded to a shared (secure) site for later download and knowledge sharing within the company.

6   Field Evaluation Results

The evaluation of the 'Digital Peer-Tutoring' learning format consisted of weekly evaluations after each of the four sessions, and a final evaluation with participation from all key stakeholders. Here, we report about the initial results from the final evaluation; a one-day meeting in the location of the factory of the case company. The participants in the evaluation were all those present at the upstart meeting 6 weeks before. They were: company managers (Company manager J and Company manager K), learning format users (Worker Br, Worker H, Worker Bi), corporate learning consultant (corporate learning consultant F), educational institution teacher(s) (Teacher J, Teacher T), pilot project manager(s) (Teacher T, Teacher J), pilot project documentarist (Documentarist F), and a digital competence facilitator (Digital competence facilitator S).

The initial results from the final evaluation reveal both short- and long-term benefits and challenges of Digital Peer-Tutoring.

6.1   Short Term Benefits

The workers liked the learning format and found it useful: *"…worker-video on iPad [could be useful]…"*, [Worker Br]. This confirms previous findings on the usefulness of video [11], and extends it to the shop floor workers.

However, the workers found that the instruction videos were too long and complicated. *"[They should be cut down to a list of four points"* [Worker Br]. Too long videos can be an expression of an 'apathetic ethical stance', a stance that reduces the worker-user to be a mean of input for the intended final design [18].

On the other hand, the workers expressed that they could use video to both think about a problem, sketch different solutions, and evaluate their use: *"Sketches …. I had read up on it, go and think about it…."* [Worker Br], and *"the worker should be able to pause the video …"* [Worker Bi]. Thus, there were indications that the format helped workers explore new technologies from an emphatic ethical user – that is, from their own – perspective [18]. Company manager K supported this: *"We, as a business must spend more time on [workers' use of video to innovate]."* The management perspective adds a new layer to understand short term benefits of video-sketching and ethical design, and thus center our focus on the multi-layered essence of user experiences at work.

6.2   Long-Term Benefits

The stakeholders also commented on the long-term benefits of the learning format:

1. The format could be used to tackle issues in the manufacturing, as *"help videos"* [Worker Bi], and a *"Company database of videos that could be accessed even years after production"* [Company manager J],

2. New employees could be introduced to the job: *"A new one that is totally novice [could use worker-created-how-to-videos]"* [Company manager J],
3. Help dyslexic employees who could watch how to do things, rather than read,
4. Supplier courses could be made memorable by *"record[ing] what the supplier shows on the shop floor"* [Corporate learning consultant F], and *"Cut out what is not useful [from the supplier teaching]"* [Company manager K]
5. Starting new ways to produce, for example *"recording the results from the company's informal and formal experiments on the shop floor"* [Company manager J, Company manager K], and *"recording order-specific ideas for how-to, so next time this order comes in, the video shows what to do"* [Worker Bi], and *"The video can be used to "squeeze" a good idea out of an experienced employee who will have to think a little about the idea"* [Teacher T].
6. Finally, the stakeholder group discussed that the learning format could also be used to produce videos for customers for marketing purposes and quality documentation.

These benefits allude to a diversity of user experiences in work situations, and perhaps tell us that the ethical stances taken by workers-as-designers-of-their-own-work may be confounded by management's strategic interest in how-to knowledge.

7 Discussion and Conclusion

We conclude that our proposed Digital Peer-Tutoring learning format enabled shop floor workers to design positive UXs for themselves and their colleagues, and beyond ways that we expected. The participating shop floor workers stated in various ways that they liked the Digital Peer-tutoring how-to videos and found them useful. This corresponds to the claim made by Twidale [17] that it is possible to use peer tutoring to give informal technical help between colleagues, and with Ørngreen et al. [11] who suggest to link various sketching techniques and creative reflection processes to video productions. The videos helped workers create ideas about robot use, identify problems not formulated before, sketch alternatives, test solutions, and demonstrate them to colleagues.

Company owners, management, and workers had unexpected ideas about how to use the peer-tutoring videos within and outside the company, in for example internal quality control and customer communication. Thus, similar to the point made about peer tutoring [13], we should acknowledge the role of Digital Peer-Tutoring in developing problem solving skills at various organizational levels.

Based on the categories proposed in [18], we furthermore observe that the ethical stance built into the 'Digital Peer-Tutoring' learning format can be characterized as 'apathetic', when too long and complex instructional videos, intended to teach workers' design thinking and enabling their own video-production, tend to make workers give up. However, the learning format also showed to be 'empathetic', as workers produced their own videos and evaluated solutions together, effectively co-designing work procedures.

We developed the Digital Peer-Tutoring learning format to improve workers' capability to create and share solutions to human-robot collaboration challenges in SMEs. Thereby we also answer the call for research into how SMEs can adopt and implement new technologies that build upon and enhance worker capabilities, skills, and knowledge [3, 6].

References

1. Draxler, S., Stevens, G.: Supporting the collaborative appropriation of an open software ecosystem. Comput. Support. Coop. Work **20**(4–5), 403–448 (2011). https://doi.org/10.1007/s10606-011-9148-9
2. Hague, A.C., Benest, I.D.: Towards over-the-shoulder guidance following a traditional learning metaphor. Comput. Educ. **26**(1–3), 61–70 (1996)
3. Hannola, L., Richter, A., Richter, S., Stocker, A.: Empowering production workers with digitally facilitated knowledge processes–a conceptual framework. Int. J. Prod. Res. (2018). https://doi.org/10.1080/00207543.2018.1445877
4. Kolko, J.: Abductive thinking and sensemaking: the drivers of design synthesis. Des. Issues **26**(1), 15–28 (2010). https://doi.org/10.1162/desi.2010.26.1.15
5. Kragic, D., Gustafson, J., Karaoguz, H., Jensfelt, P., Krug, R.: Interactive, collaborative robots: challenges and opportunities (2017). https://www.ijcai.org/proceedings/2018/0003.pdf. Accessed 19 May 2019
6. Ludwig, T., Kotthaus, C., Stein, M., Pipek, V., Wulf, V.: Revive Old Discussions! Socio-technical Challenges for Small and Medium Enterprises within Industry 4.0. In: Proceedings of 16th European Conference on Computer-Supported Cooperative Work (2018). https://doi.org/10.18420/ecscw2018_15
7. Magin, D.J., Churches, A.E.: Peer tutoring in engineering design: a case study. Stud. High. Educ. **20**(1), 73–85 (1995)
8. Martinez, J., Harris, C., Jalali, C., Tung, J., Meyer, R.: Using peer-assisted learning to teach and evaluate residents' musculoskeletal skills. Med. Educ. Online **20**(1), 27255 (2015)
9. Mucha, H., Büttner, S., Röcker, C.: Application areas for human-centered assistive systems. In: Human-Computer Interaction–Perspectives on Industry 4.0. Workshop at i-KNOW 2016 Graz, Austria, October 2016 (2016.)
10. Murphy-Hill, E., Lee, D.Y., Murphy, G.C., McGrenere, J.: How Do Users Discover New Tools in Software Development and Beyond? Computer Supported Cooperative Work (CSCW) **24**(5), 389–422 (2015). https://doi.org/10.1007/s10606-015-9230-9
11. Ørngreen, R., Henningsen, B., Gundersen, P., Hautopp, H.: The learning potential of video sketching. In: Proceedings of the 16th European Conference on elearning ISCAP Porto, Portugal, 26–27 October 2017, pp. 422–430 (2017)
12. Sanchez-Tamayo, N., Wachs, J.P.: Collaborative robots in surgical research: a low-cost adaptation. In: Companion of the 2018 ACM/IEEE International Conference on Human-Robot Interaction, pp. 231–232 (2018)
13. Schleyer, G.K., Langdon, G.S., James, S.: Peer tutoring in conceptual design. Eur. J. Eng. Educ. **30**(2), 245–254 (2005)
14. Schulz, R.: Collaborative robots learning spatial language for picking and placing objects on a table. In: Proceedings of the 5th International Conference on Human Agent Interaction, pp. 329–333 (2017)
15. Secomb, J.: A systematic review of peer teaching and learning in clinical education. J. Clin. Nurs. **17**(6), 703–716 (2008)
16. Sein, M.K., Henfridsson, O., Sandeep, P., Rossi, M., Lindgren, R.: Action design research. MIS Q. **35**(1), 37–56 (2011). https://doi.org/10.2307/23043488
17. Twidale, M.B.: Over the shoulder learning: supporting brief informal learning. Comput. Support. Coop. Work **14**(6), 505–547 (2005)
18. Vistisen, P., Jensen, T., Poulsen, S.B.: Animating the ethical demand: exploring user dispositions in industry innovation cases through animation-based sketching. ACM SIGCAS Comput. Soc. **45**(3), 318–325 (2016)

Proposed System for a Socio-Technical Design Framework for Improved User Collaborations with Automation Technologies

Parisa Saadati[1]([⊠]) [iD], José Abdelnour-Nocera[1,2] [iD], and Torkil Clemmensen[3] [iD]

[1] University of West London, London, UK
{parisa.saadati,abdejos}@uwl.ac.uk
[2] ITI/Larsys, Funchal, Portugal
[3] Copenhagen Business School, Frederiksberg, Denmark
tc.digi@cbs.dk

Abstract. To improve human performance, interactive technologies are going towards more automated systems that involve computers, robots and cyber-physical systems into the decision-making process. While automation can lead to increased performance and reduced impact of human errors, interactive technologies without optimal design can have a negative impact on the experience of operators and end-users, leading to suboptimal performance of the automated systems. In this research, we aim to evaluate and refine Human Work Interaction Design (HWID) framework to be applicable in various highly-automated settings including Industry 4.0 environments. This will be performed via a thorough literature review as the first step. The list of identified factors playing a potential role in various interactive systems will then be evaluated and optimised in three case studies. We will try to understand how to maximise collaborations between the users and the machine in interactive systems. A practical approach for evaluating both employees' and end-users' perspectives in three scenarios with different levels of automation will be assessed. We will evaluate the outputs in multiple levels of organisations, employees and end-users. The ultimate output of the study will be a framework or model that will help in designing future research studies for various automation scenarios, especially semi-autonomous systems that involve high levels of interaction between users and the machine. We will provide guidelines for implementation of the proposed framework in different scenarios. We expect that the framework output of this research will provide a comprehensive guideline applicable to many Industry 4.0 technologies.

Keywords: Sociotechnical · Human work interaction design · Automation · Augmentation · Industry 4.0

1 Introduction

During the life cycle of any organisation, a variety of environmental stimuli will influence its operations and decision-making processes. These external factors are dependent

© IFIP International Federation for Information Processing 2020
Published by Springer Nature Switzerland AG 2020
J. Abdelnour Nocera et al. (Eds.): INTERACT 2019, LNCS 11930, pp. 59–67, 2020.
https://doi.org/10.1007/978-3-030-46540-7_7

on economic and social factors, political and legislative changes, and developments in technology and human knowledge. The internal environment may also influence various processes and elements of an organisation such as the staff, information and monitoring systems or management policies [1]. Complex organisational systems inevitably rely now on large-scale software-intensive systems. In this paper, we hint at a possible sociotechnical HCI framework with customized value propositions and a case presentation for a future investigation of three different scenarios with different levels of automation.

Socio-Technical System Design (STSD) developments have identified and addressed several problems in understanding and developing complex systems. Despite many positive outcomes, these methods have not materially changed industrial software engineering practices. One of the main reasons behind this is involving users only in the testing stage of any new system development instead of the design process [2].

Currently, 'automation' is one of the main means for supporting operators using systems that feature high complexity. Automation allows designers to transfer the burden from operators to machine by re-allocating the system tasks that were previously performed by human [3]. Researchers have studied different aspects of implementation of advanced interactive technologies employing automation in different platforms [1, 3–7].

Organisations can now improve operations and decision making by implementing cyber-physical systems (CPS) and internet of things (IoT), and potentially linking them to blockchain technology in the future. Rising integration of Internet of Everything (IoE) into the industrial value chain is the foundation of "Industry 4.0" technologies [8]. These technologies can improve the end-users' experience via increasing the self-service options, optimising operations and security processes, and enhancing ground asset management and connectivity.

An important point to consider is that implementing new technologies in a complex service-driven work environment (e.g. an airport terminal) does not necessarily and automatically guarantee a positive response from workers and customers [9]. Hence, developments towards future 'smart workplaces' need to be carefully designed in order to achieve expected service quality goals for both end-users and employees. The main purpose of this study is to identify all humanistic/social and technological elements in the design of newly automated systems applicable to Industry 4.0 that are affecting the human and machine collaborations. This paper is organised as follows. Section 2 introduces the findings of the literature review on different factors affecting the human and machine collaborations and categorising them into three main categories. Section 3 proposes the future research outcome by investigating into these factors from three case studies; university library, research platform and an airport.

2 Review

Automating a process that is embedded into people's everyday lives will surely impact their experience. Automation replaces or rearranges people's practices and habits that may have been developed over long periods. Therefore, using automation in interactive systems requires consideration of potential changes on human activity and the new coordination demands on the human operators. These experiences highly depend on the type and level of automation [7] and to what extent the developer has allowed the machine to make decisions.

2.1 Technological Elements of Interactive Systems

Around 1970 s and after a series of technological advances labelled as the third industrial revolution (also called "the digital revolution"), the transition towards the fourth industrial revolution (Industry 4.0) is now undergoing that will transform the design, manufacturing, and operation of various products and systems [7]. The increasing integration of the Internet of Everything (IoE) into the industrial value chain has built the foundation for this revolution [8]. The increased connectivity and interaction among systems, humans and machines support the integration of various automated or semi-automated systems, and hence, increasing flexibility and productivity [10]. These automated systems will lead to interconnected manufacturing systems and supply chains with their own challenges.

To achieve sufficient autonomous awareness in a system, efficient integration of smart sensors and mobile devices is required alongside industrial communication protocols and standards. Economic impact of this industrial revolution is supposed to be huge [10], as it promises substantial increase in operational effectiveness as well as the development of new business models, services, products and organisational structures and culture [10–12].

Three key components of Industry 4.0 are Internet of Things (IoT), Cyber-Physical Systems (CPS), and smart workplaces. The main objects commonly used in the Industry 4.0 are RFID (radio-frequency identifiers), sensors, actuators, and mobile phones that interacts with each other and cooperate with their neighbouring smart components to reach the common goal. For all these smart objects and people who are going to collaborate with them, there is a need for setting technical standards to enable them to work.

Industry 4.0 advancements [7] are categorised into 4 main principles in general:

1. Technical assistance,
2. Interconnections,
3. Decentralised decisions, and
4. Information transparency.

The main focus of this research will be on the "Collaborations" sub-principle of the "Interconnections" principle (which includes Collaborations, Standards and Security).

Three type of collaborations are considered in the context of Industry 4.0: human-human, human-machine and machine-machine collaborations. As a result of recent advances in smart interactive systems, employees' experience and access to technology have increased substantially. Recent development of using smart technologies in new domains such as health, education, finance and the impact of Industry 4.0 technologies in manufacturing and logistics have raised new challenges for Human Computer Interaction (HCI) researchers and practitioners.

2.2 Human Work Interaction Design

Human Work Interaction Design (HWID) is a comprehensive framework that aims to establish relationships between extensive empirical work-domain studies and HCI designs. It builds on the foundation of Cognitive Work Analysis (CWA) [5]. HWID is currently positioned as a modern lightweight version of CWA.

HWID studies how to understand, conceptualise, and design for the complex and emergent contexts in which information and communication technologies (ICT) and work are entangled [1]. HWID models are based on the characteristics of humans and work domain contents and the interactions during their tasks and decision making activities (Fig. 1). HWID focuses on the integration of work analysis (i.e., CWA methods) and interaction design methods (e.g. goal-oriented design and HCI usability) for smart workplaces. The ultimate goal of HWID is to empower users by designing smarter workplaces in various work domains.

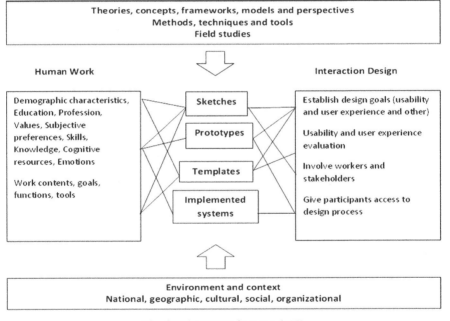

Fig. 1. The HWID framework [5]

For applying HWID models to specific workplaces we need to consider several independent and entangled factors [5]. Considering numerous theories, concepts, techniques and methods developed for other work environments is the first step. Environmental contexts such as national, cultural, geographic, social and organisational factors will have an important role in designing optimal HWID models, as they impact interaction between users (i.e. both operators and employees) and smart systems in their work and life. There are more work-related factors including the users' knowledge/skills, application domain, work contents and goals, as well as the nature of tasks or newly introduced technologies to be considered in the interaction performance. Developing HWID models requires establishing design goals, evaluation of usability and user experience, engagement of all stakeholders, and provision of transparent design processes.

2.3 Smart Workplace

"Smart Workplace" is a vision where the organisation is fully connected with all stakeholders via proactive adaptation to the real-time needs of the organisation including operational necessities and customer requests. As an example, security concerns in airports necessitate more investigations prior to the boarding, which results in long queues and waiting times for passengers. Hence, airports need to be more innovative in operations and handling of stakeholders (passengers and workers) and their needs in real time.

2.4 Humanistic Elements of Interactive Systems

To address human element in designing complex interactive systems, design fiction and design ethnography should be linked [13]. This is in line with considering the impact of anthropology on the design's future-orientedness by understanding the cultural meanings and sensitivity to values and context [14]. Analysis of the allocation of functions is necessary to identify the optimal distribution of both functions and tasks between a partly-autonomous system and the user [3].

Physical support of human workers by robots or machines is an important aspect of new technologies. This is due to involvement of users in conducting a range of tasks that are unpleasant, too exhausting or unsafe [15, 16]. For an effective, successful, and safe support of users in physical tasks, it is necessary that robots or machines interact smoothly and intuitively with their human counterparts [15], and that humans are properly trained for this kind of human-machine collaboration [8].

The Value of Information. In collaborations between human and machine, the value of information is now more recognised given high power of the machine in decision-making in highly-automated systems. For instance, informing users about the sensor's reading power of Tesla's automated car can significantly increase their trust [6]. However, other studies show that the number of information items or tasks users receive in an automated process should be personalised and up to the point of their desire/tolerability. Not enough functions allocated to a user will lead to underload and boredom and thus decreased performance. [17] Too many allocated functions will lead to cognitive, perceptive or motoric overload and increase negative emotions (e.g. stress, anxiety) [18] and user's error. [3, 17] Meanwhile, users can cope with emotions after spending some time with the autonomous technology and developing some routines.

Providing an abundance of information and transparency is an important hypothesis in interactive technologies. Trust, transparency and acceptance of losing control (i.e. shared authority between the user and system [8]) can improve the interaction of the user by revealing the ambiguous feelings toward the automation. Other psychological factors under study include worries about practical challenges and security of the technology (e.g. hacking a system) and reliability of the process itself (e.g. flat mobile phone battery for systems that rely on applications). Users may lose their trust in decision-making of an automated system when other humans who will not follow the same process are involved and can impact on the outcome (e.g. if fishermen not using a specific application access to more fish than those using that application).

An important situation is when responsibilities are shared between users and the system. Ability to identify responsible party related to a bad outcome (i.e. user error versus system failure) can impact the performance of users [9]. Controllable designed interface and environment of work, as well as feeling safe while using new technologies, are among other factors that can increase the performance of the users.

Involving Users in the Design Process. The design process should determine the content and format of information to be shared with users in order to create an experience of certainty and trust. Feedback from the users plays a major role for designing such systems. However, the amount and format of the feedback must be well chosen, otherwise it might question the main advantage of automation itself.

Research needs to bridge the gap between the micro-perspective of technology specifications and the macro-perspective of how life will and should change through implementation of that technology. Enacting future systems "in the wild", as a particular form of prototyping, is certainly an important element of this bridge.

Motivating the users to engage with the new technologies is still a challenge due to lack of understanding of the end-users' individual experience and interaction with such technologies. Users can have different roles or backgrounds that can affect their discovery, collaboration and learning of the interactive system [11]. Researchers have tried to recruit users for testing their interaction via use of flyers or instructions explaining the technology (a process known as augmentation) [19].

Furthermore, engaging users in designing the automated or augmented product will change their interaction time. The development teams need to familiarise themselves with space and environment of practices, build trust with the employees and improve design ideas. Studies suggest the relations between modes of discovery, design improvements, interaction and socio-spatial aspects. These relations can be developed more as an analytical and design tool to redefine the borders of opportunities for social interaction in daily automated spaces.

2.5 Summary of the Review

We believe that there are unmet needs for evaluation and identification of both technical and humanistic factors involved in partly-autonomous systems [3, 7]. Unlike the extensive technical literature on automation, there is a small research base examining the human capabilities involved in work with automated systems [7].

Several factors such as sociological and psychological exchanges, ergonomic, cultural relativity, technology availability and acceptance, etc., have been proposed to be involved in human-machine collaboration in various settings, especially in higher levels of automation. However, the main problem is that there is no comprehensive list of these factors, and no previous study has tried to develop a model based on these factors. Such a model will be helpful to system designers for developing any new interactive highly-automated system.

We therefore see HWID framework as a funnel for socio-technical design, automation technologies, and information system (Fig. 2).

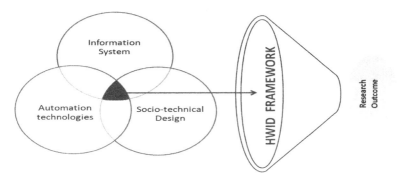

Fig. 2. Main scopes of proposed HWID research on user collaboration with automation in complex settings

3   Proposed Further Research

For investigating independent and entangled factors related to human and machine collaborations in automated systems, we propose a practical approach for evaluating both end-users' and employees' (or operators') perspectives in an automatous environment.

First step (current stage) in this research is to produce a list of relevant factors from different sources including: review of the relevant literature, contact and interview with experts in this domain, and observation of some smart workplaces. This comprehensive list will then be evaluated and optimised in two scenarios (scenario 1, University of West London Library, and scenario 2, Indian Research Platform). These scenarios were selected carefully based on potentially important factors including socio-behavioural (e.g., work pattern), psychological (e.g., trust in system), demographical (e.g., wealth and ethnicity), and geographical characteristics of their user populations.

We will analyse previously available (via literature review and expert opinions) and newly-gathered data (via questionnaires and interviews) to produce a model to be validated onscenario 3 settings (i.e., London based airport). By several iterations in this highly automated environment we will refine and provide the final output of the study, which will be a tool/guideline for designing HWID models for various interactive technologies. Figure 3 below depicts the proposed process of research in this study.

Given the variety of environments and different levels of automation, we will potentially achieve different lists of factors that affect the performance of both operators and systems. This will help us to update the list for different environments. In the final scenario, current shortcomings and future opportunities will be evaluated by using an HWID model for future smart workplaces using Industry 4.0 framework.

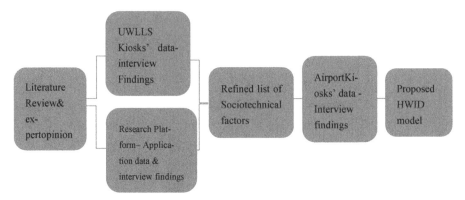

Fig. 3. Research procedure

4 Conclusion

In summary, the overall objective of this paper was to present a review of the possible theoretical background for a to-be-developed sociotechnical HCI framework, including customized value propositions for the work domain of choice, and, finally, to present three scenarios to be considered in future research. One of the outcomes that the current stage is a comprehensive list category in main principle and number of sub-principles of the factors impact the machine and human counterpart collaboration from sociotechnical perspective. This is what we hoped to illustrate with this paper as start of a series of papers in different scenarios with various automation level.

References

1. Kulju, M., Ylikauppila, M., Toivonen, S., Salmela, L.: A framework for understanding human factors issues in border control automation. In: Barricelli, B.R., et al. (eds.) HWID 2018. IAICT, vol. 544, pp. 215–228. Springer, Cham (2019). https://doi.org/10.1007/978-3-030-05297-3_15
2. Baxter, G., Sommerville, I.: Socio-technical systems: from design methods to systems engineering. Interact. Comput. **23**(1), 4–17 (2011). https://doi.org/10.1016/j.intcom.2010.07.003
3. Bouzekri, E., Canny, A., Martinie, C., Palanque, P., Gris, C.: Using task descriptions with explicit representation of allocation of functions, authority and responsibility to design and assess automation. In: Barricelli, B.R., et al. (eds.) HWID 2018. IAICT, vol. 544, pp. 36–56. Springer, Cham (2019). https://doi.org/10.1007/978-3-030-05297-3_3
4. Abdelnour-Nocera, J., Oussena, S., Burns, C.: Human work interaction design of the smart university. In: Abdelnour Nocera, J., Barricelli, B.R., Lopes, A., Campos, P., Clemmensen, T. (eds.) HWID 2015. IAICT, vol. 468, pp. 127–140. Springer, Cham (2015). https://doi.org/10.1007/978-3-319-27048-7_9
5. Clemmensen, T.: A human work interaction design (HWID) case study in e-government and public information systems. Int. J. Public Inf. Syst. **3**, 105–113 (2011)
6. Dikmen, M., Burns, C.: Trust in autonomous vehicles. In: 2017 IEEE International Conference on Systems, Man, and Cybernetics, pp. 1093–1098 (2017). https://doi.org/10.1109/SMC.2017.8122757

7. Parasuraman, R., Sheridan, T., Wickens, C.: A model for types and level of human interaction with automation. IEEE Trans. Syst. Man Cybern. - Part A Syst. Hum. **30**(3), 286–297 (2000)
8. Hermann, M., Pentek, T., Otto, B.: Design Principles for Industrie 4.0 Scenarios, pp. 3928–3937. IEEE (2016). http://doi.10.1109/HICSS.2016.48
9. World Economic Forum: The fourth Industrial Revolution (2018). https://www.weforum.org/pages/the-fourth-industrial-revolution-by-klaus-schwab. Accessed 22 Aug 2018
10. Davies, R.: Industry 4.0: Digitalisation for productivity and growth. European Parliamentary Research Service (2015)
11. Lesser, E., Prusak, L.: Communities of practice, social capital and organizational knowledge. Inf. Syst. Rev. **1**, 3–10 (1999). http://providersedge.com/docs/km_articles/Cop_-_Social_Capital_-_Org_K.pdf. Accessed 25 Feb 2019
12. International Airport reviews. https://www.internationalairportreview.com/article/25929/personalisation-smart-airport/. Accessed 18 Feb 2019
13. Lindley, J., Sharma, D., Potts, R.: Anticipatory ethnography: design fiction as an input to design ethnography. In: Ethnographic Praxis in Industry Conference Proceedings 2014, pp. 237–253 (2014). https://doi.org/10.1111/1559-8918.01030
14. Otto, T., Smith, R.C., Gunn, W.: Design Anthropology: A Distinct Style of Knowing, pp. 1–29. Bloomsbury, London (2013)
15. Awais, M., Henrich, D.: Human-robot interaction in an unknown human intention scenario. In: 11th International Conference on Frontiers of Information Technology, 2013, pp. 89–94 (2013). https://doi.org/10.1109/FIT.2013.24
16. Kiesler, S. Hinds, P.: Human-Robot Interaction. Human-Computer Interaction, vol. 19 (2004)
17. Yerkes, R.M., Dodson, J.D.: The relation of strength of stimulus to rapidly of habit- formation. J. Comp. Neurol. Psychol. **18**(5), 459–482 (1908)
18. Kirk, A., Brown, D.F.: Employee assistance programs: a review of the management of stress and wellbeing through workplace counselling and consulting. Aust. Psychol. **38**(2), 138–143 (2003)
19. Wouters, N., et al.: Uncovering the honeypot effect: how audiences engage with public interactive systems. In: Proceedings of the 2016 ACM Conference on Designing Interactive Systems, pp. 5–16. ACM (2016). http://doi.org/10.1145/2901790.2901796

Workshop on Handling Security, Usability, User Experience and Reliability in User-Centered Development Processes

Assessing the Performance of Agile Teams

Marta Kristin Larusdottir$^{(\boxtimes)}$ (iD) and Marcel Kyas (iD)

Reykjavik University, Menntavegur 1, 102 Reykjavik, Iceland
{marta,marcel}@ru.is

Abstract. Selecting a well performing agile software development team to develop a particular software is a complex issue for public authorities. This selection is often based on the estimated total cost of the project in an official request for proposals. In this paper we describe an alternative approach where three performance factors and the estimated cost were assessed and weighted to find the best agile team for a particular project. Five agile software development teams that fulfilled predefined technical requirements were invited to take part in one day workshops. The public authority involved wanted to assess both how each team performed during the workshops and the quality of the deliverables they handed in. The three performance factors were: (1) team collaboration and user experience focus, (2) user stories delivery and (3) the quality of the code. We describe the process of assessing the three performance factors during and after the workshops and the results of the assessments. The team that focused on one user story during the workshop and emphasized the three different quality factors, user experience, accessibility and security, got the highest rating from the assessment and were selected for the project. We also describe the lessons learned after concluding the assessment.

Keywords: User experience · Accessibility · Security · Agile development · Team collaboration · Agile teams

1 Introduction

When public authorities want to make new software systems to be used by citizens and employees for solving various tasks they often negotiate with software companies for developing the software. The selection of the software company for making the software needs to be free and open for competition according to European Union legislation, so the public authorities must issue a public request for proposal (RTF). Typically the RTF contains two sections: (1) the requirements and needs for the system to be developed, and (2) the selection criteria [12]. Often the selection criteria is based on the cost solely, so the software companies estimate the hours needed to be able to develop the software fulfilling the requirements and needs stated. The company with the lowest prize gets the job [12]. In a case study of four software companies in Denmark developing for public authorities, the software companies focused on what the public authorities are willing to pay for and what they wanted to citizens to be able to do [2]. So the software

© IFIP International Federation for Information Processing 2020
Published by Springer Nature Switzerland AG 2020
J. Abdelnour Nocera et al. (Eds.): INTERACT 2019, LNCS 11930, pp. 71–83, 2020.
https://doi.org/10.1007/978-3-030-46540-7_8

companies did not include quality factors like user experience (UX) or security issues, in their proposal, if it was not requested in the RFT.

In some cases the selection criteria is based on both the prize and quality factors, so the price could weight 60% and the quality criteria 40% for example [12]. Requirements for quality factors, like user experience (UX) and security, can be included in the requirement section of the RTF defining the level of the UX and security in the developed system. The requirements can also be included in the selection criteria, defining how much weight in the selection process the UX and security factors have [22]. Typically, the usage of particular methods like user testing and the frequency of using those methods would be stated in the selection criteria. Another option would be that the public authority may state performance criteria for the users, for example that the users will be able to accomplish a particular task within a particular time limit [22]. One possibility is to base the selection criteria on the competences of the software team getting the job, but that is not frequently done. The selection criteria should state the wanted knowledge, skills and competences of the team, in that case. Possibly, the criteria could also include the focus on quality aspects that the team should have. In any case, the objective of the process is to find the best team for the job according the predefined criteria and thereby get the best outcome for the money spent.

There are many aspects that affect a project outcome. A study of four similar software teams developing software to fit the same needs, described 1 to 6 variation in the prizes of the outcome [21]. The teams were similar in technical competences. The quality of the outcome was also assessed and the team with the next lowest price scored best on the three quality aspects in the study, usability, maintainability and reliability. That team had one project manager, one developer and one interaction designer in the team, but the other teams had two developers and one project manager. The best team used intermediate process models for the development, with analysis and design in the first four weeks, then implementation from week 4 to 10 and testing in the last six weeks of the project [21].

In this paper we describe an approach, where the performance of five agile software development teams was evaluated as a part of the selection criteria for selecting the best agile team for making a web service. The performance factors included: (1) team collaboration and user experience focus, (2) user stories delivered and (3) quality of code including accessibility and security. The performance factors were assessed during and after a one day workshop with the team, where the teams were observed and their deliverables reviewed. The performance factors weighted 70% and the cost 30% in the selection criteria for the best agile team.

2   Related Work on the Performance Factors

In this section we briefly describe the related literature on the performance factors evaluated in this study. First we give a brief overview of agile development and team collaboration, we explain the format and usage of user stories and then we briefly describe the concept of user experience and code quality.

2.1 Agile Development and Team Collaboration

The agile process Scrum [20] has gained popularity in the software industry in recent years. According to an international survey, Scrum was the most popular process of the agile processes with more than 50% of the IT professionals surveyed were using it [23]. A similar trend is seen in the software industry in Iceland, but the lean process Kanban [17] has also been gaining popularity lately [15].

A characteristic of Scrum is the observation that small, cross-functional teams historically produce the best results. Scrum is based on a rugby metaphor in which the team's contribution is more important than each individual con-tri-bution. Scrum teams typically consists of people with three major roles: (1) a Scrum Master that acts as project manager/buffer to the outside world; (2) a Product Owner that represents stakeholders, and (3) a team of developers (less than 10). One of the twelve principles behind the agile manifesto is: "The most efficient and effective method of conveying information to and within a development team is face-to-face conversation." [16]. In agile development the teams should collaborate openly and all the team is responsible for delivering a potentially shippable product after each sprint.

Some of the more important artifacts and ceremonies with-in Scrum is the Sprint, which defines 15–30 days iteration, the Product backlog of requirements described by user stories and managed by the Product Owner and the Daily Scrum meeting, which is the daily meeting for the team and the Scrum Master to plan the work of the day and report what was done the day before [20].

2.2 User Stories

In Scrum, the user requirements are usually described by user stories. The most common format for describing a user story is: "As a [user role], I want to [do some task] to [achieve a goal]" [4]. The user stories are used to describe the requirements for the whole system being developed kept in the Product Backlog. During the Sprint planning meeting, the team, the Scrum Master and the Product Owner select the user stories that the team will work on during the next sprint in accordance to how many user stories it is possible to implement during the time of a sprint. The Product Owner describes the priorities of the user stories, so the most important user stories will be selected for the particular sprint according to the Product Owners criterias. During the daily Scrum meeting, the team members report what user stories and tasks they will be working on during the day and what the finished they day before.

2.3 User Experience

UX has gained momentum in computer science and is defined in the ISO 9241-210 in the following way [10]: "Person's perceptions and responses resulting from the use and/or anticipated use of a product, system or service". Researchers agree that UX is a complex concept, including aspects like fun, pleasure, beauty and personal growth. An experience is subjective, holistic, situated, dynamic, and worthwhile [8]. A recent survey on what practitioner's think is included in the term UX shows that respondents agreed that user-related factors, contextual factors and temporal dynamics of UX are all important factors for defining the term UX [14]. The temporal dynamic of UX also reached consensus amongst the respondents.

Many methods have been suggested for active participation of users in the software development process with the aim of developing software with good user experience. Some of the methods for focusing on either the expected UX or the UX after users have used a particular system, including interviews with users, surveys, observations and user testing [19]. IT professionals rated formal user testing as the most useful method for active participation of users in their software development for understanding the UX of the developed system [11].

2.4 Quality of Code Including Security and Accessibility

Code quality is generally hard to define objectively. Desirable characteristics include reliability, performance efficiency, security, and maintainability [5]. Metrics to assess code quality usually include volume of code, redundancy, unit size, complexity, unit interface size, and coupling [1, 9]. The process of measuring properties like complexity and the decision on what unit size is acceptable depend on the context and is often subjective.

Accessibility of web application is typically realized by conforming to the WCAG 2.0 recommendation [3]. Following these recommendation allows a web page to be interpreted and processed by accessibility software. For example, by a.o. preferring relative font sizes over absolute ones allows the web page to be rendered in any font size and making it accessible to users with visual impairments. The WCAG is seen as an important part of making web pages accessible [13].

Indeed, for any web application and any mobile application used by the public sector in the European Economic Area must conform to the WCAG [6].

3   The Case - The Financial Support RTF

Reykjavik city has decided to make the digital services easy to use for all the citizens of Reykjavik. The motivation came from two new employees that wanted to change the web services to being more user centered. One of the first projects for this attempt had the objective to make the application for financial support more usable to citizens, but to focus also on security and reliability of the code. An official request for proposals was made to select "the best" team for taking part in developing a web service in collaboration with IT professionals at Reykjavik city. One of the constraints was that the team had to follow an agile development process similar to Scrum, by using user stories, conducting daily Scrum meetings and focus on the values of agile team work and collaboration.

The teams that submitted a proposal were evaluated according minimal technical requirements and their performance and delivery after a one day workshop. There were five steps in the selection process: (a) First the team submitted a proposal, (b) The applying teams were evaluated according to the minimum technical requirements, (c) the teams fulfilling the technical requirements were assessed according to performance criteria, (d) the hourly prices of each team member were evaluated and (e) the final selection of a team was decided. In this section we describe the minimal technical requirements for the teams and the three performance factors assessed during and after the one day workshops.

3.1 The Minimal Technical Requirements

The minimal technical requirements were described in the request for proposals document. The teams had to provide at least 5 team members, whereof at least:

1. Two members had to be skilled backend programmers, which had experience in writing code that was tested for security. For confirming these skills, the team members were asked to deliver a list of projects were they had worked on security issues for the system. They also had to list at least 5 software projects that they had been involved in. They had to be experienced in automated testing and have knowledge of .NET programming.
2. 1 member had to be a user interface programmer. This persons had to have the experience of making apps or web services that fulfilled the accessibility standard, European Norm EN 301 549 V1.1.2 [7] that includes the WCAG 2.0 Level A and Level AA and are scalable for all major smart equipment and computers. This person had to describe his/her involvement in five software development projects.
3. 1 member had to be interaction designer or a UX specialist. This member had to have taken part in developing at least 5 software systems, (apps or web services), with at least 100 users each. They should describe their experience of user centered design with direct contact with users and what methods they had used to integrate user in the development.
4. 1 member should had to be an agile coach or a Scrum Master. To fulfill this, the person had to have led at least one team with at least three members with at least 10 two week sprints. This member should describe his experience regarding coaching team members.

3.2 The Workshop Organization

Five teams fulfilled the above minimum technical requirements. Each of them were invited for a one day performance workshop. The workshops took place at an office at the IT department of Reykjavik city in October and November 2018. The teams got four user stories to as possible tasks to work on during the workshop.

The user stories were the following:

1. *As a* citizen of Reykjavik that has impaired intellectual ability *I want to be able to* apply for financial assistance via web/mobile *so that* I can apply in an simple and easy-to-understand manner.
2. *As a* employee of Reykjavik city with little tech know-how *I want to be able to* see all applications in a "employee interface" *so that* I have a good overview of all applications that have been sent.

3. *As a* Reykjavík city employee which is colorblind *I want to be able to* send the result of the application process to the applicant *so that* the applicant can know as soon as possible if the applicant is eligible for financial assistance.
4. *As a* audit authority for financial assistance *I want to be able to* see who has viewed applications *so that* I can perform my audit responsibility.

The workshops were organized by a project manager at Reykjavik city. The schedule was the following:

1. The team got a one hour introduction to the schedule of the day and to the work environment at Reykjavik city, the services and systems, the organization and work practices. Also the user stories were introduced briefly.
2. The teams were asked to do a daily Scrum meeting for 15 min for selecting the tasks for the day and to organize the day for 15 min. The experts focusing on team collaboration and UX focus observed this part of the workshops.
3. The teams worked on developing their deliverables during the day.
4. The last 45 min of the day, the teams were asked to present to all the involved experts and the organizing team, their work practices and their deliverables. The teams could plan these 45 min as they preferred. They had been introduced to the performance factors that were being assessed, so some of the teams deliberately organized the presentation according to these factors.

3.3 The Performance Factors Assessed During and After the Workshops

The workshops had the goal of assessing the following three performance factors:

1. The teams collaboration and user experience (UX) focus
2. Their delivery of user stories
3. The quality of the code delivered

An assessment scheme was conducted for each of the three factors. Four external experts were asked to conduct the assessment. The team collaboration and UX focus contained four sub factors and in total these gave the maximum of 25 points. These were assessed by two external experts by observing the teams twice during the one day workshop. The delivery of user stories and the quality of the code delivered were assessed after the workshop. Two external experts in security issues and performance were asked to review the code delivered. The user stories delivered gave maximum 10 points and the quality of the code 35 points. In total these three performance factors added up to 70 points. The hourly price for the team members could give a maximum of 30 points. Experts at Reykjavik city reviewed the hourly prizes. The agile team could get 100 points in total, if they got the maximum points for all the three performance factors and the hourly prizing. We will describe the process of the data gathering for assessing the three performance factors resulting from the workshops in the next section.

4   Data Gathering for Assessing the Performance Factors

In the following we will describe the process of gathering data to be able to evaluate the team collaboration, the user stories delivered and the quality of the code.

4.1   Data Gathering for Assessing the Team Collaboration and UX Focus

Two experts in team collaboration and UX focus were asked to assess this performance factor.

Four sub factors were defined:

1. How well did the team perform at the daily meeting (max 4 points)?
2. How problem solving oriented was the team (max 8 points)?
3. How much did the team emphasize UX (user experience) (max 8 points)?
4. How well did the team present their work at the end of the workshop (max 5 points)?

The two experts observed the teams during an half an hour session in the morning, when the teams had a daily Scrum meeting and when selecting tasks for the day. The experts took notes and assessed the first sub factor. They tried to keep silent and not ask questions so the five workshops would be as similar as possible.

Forty five minutes were used as the last part of the workshop for presenting the work practices that the team used during the day and the deliverables. The two experts observed the presentation and took notes. The experts only asked, if there were issues, which the experts were about to assess, that were not mentioned during the presentation, to have better information on all the performance factors.

There was a short meetings with all the experts involved and the organizing team at Reykjavik city right after each workshop. The goal was to discuss the first impression of the workshop of that day.

For each of the sub factors there were predefined questions that the experts answered for assessing each sub factor.

For the UX emphasis sub factor, the questions were five:

(1)   Does the team emphasize UX when presenting their solution?
(2)   Does the team justify their decisions according to the needs of the users?
(3)   Does the team justify the flow and the process in the UI according to the user needs?
(4)   Has the team planned some user evaluations?
(5)   The team consulted with users during the workshop?

Each of the experts rated all the questions for the four sub factors for the teams within 48 h and noted an argument for each of the ratings. The two experts met shortly after that assessment and discussed their individual answers to the questions and the rating of each sub factor and made a consolidated rating for the team that was sent to the project manager of the workshops. When all the teams had been assessed, the two experts met to make the final comparison of all the ratings and make the final ratings that were sent to the project manager of the workshops.

4.2   Data Gathering for Assessing the User Stories Delivered

A second team of two experts was assigned the task of assessing whether the user stories had been successfully implemented. The second team had to rely on the documentation of the submission to identify the code that was supposed to implement the feature described by the user story and the test cases for that story.

Each agile team submitted their project as a dump of a git repository. Some teams also submitted sketches, mock-ups and photographs of all documentation written down during the workshop day. In addition, some teams kept a test instance of their system running for the two experts to test.

The assessment criteria were:

1. Did the submitting team make a claim that a user story was implemented? Lacking such a claim the experts would assume that the story was not implemented.
2. Did the submitting team document what functions were used to implement the user story? The experts would look at the code only for names that related to concepts in the user story.
3. Did the submitting team provide test cases to test the user story?

The verdict for each user story was pass or fail. The score was with respect to the maximum achieved by all teams. One team managed to implement 3 stories, which gave the maximum number of 10 points. All other teams scored a fraction of three, according to the number of stories they achieved. A finer distinction than pass and fail was rejected, because the experts could not agree on how that should be done objectively, and they felt that it was not worth the effort.

4.3   Data Gathering for Assessing the Quality of the Code

As mentioned above, each team submitted their code as a clone of a git repository. This enabled the experts to assess the way the teams were documenting their software development process.

The properties that the two experts assessed were:

1. Quality of the documentation in the code and description of code architecture
2. Quality of the log messages in version control
3. Quality of web accessibility
4. Error handling in the interface
5. Error handling in code
6. Functionality of the database scripts
7. Correct use of the model-view-controller pattern
8. Error free functionality

Both the experts and the City of Reykjavik believe that the quality of documentation of the code, the architecture, and the log messages in the version control system are predictors of product quality and maintainability of the resulting project.

Points 3 and 4 were most relevant to the interaction with the user. The experts used the WAVE web accessibility assessment tool to assess the quality of web accessibility and to check compliance with WCAG 2.0 at levels A and AA [7]. The experts investigated the choice of colors by hand and by using filters to simulate how color vision deficient users would see the web site. Overall, all submissions had some issues with web accessibility, like laying out information in the wrong order, missing alt tags for images, and so forth.

The two experts referred to the way erroneous behavior is conveyed by the user for assessing the error handling in the interface. The experts checked whether the error messages were displayed in a meaningful manner, how an encountered error would be addressed, and whether a pointer to assistance was provided.

The difference between error handing in the user interface and the error handling in the code was defined. If a possible user would make an error in using the system, or if the system would fail to perform the task the user wanted to achieve without being able to recover, the experts checked whether the error message delivered to the user provided a meaningful explanation of what happened and if it provided an assistance in how the user could recover from the error. If a possible error related to an internal API and could be handled programmatically, they considered it to be a code error. The experts expected such errors, typically thrown exceptions, to be caught, logged and handled.

Functionality of the data base scripts referred to how the data of the users was represented in the data model, how that model was represented as data base schemata, whether they were set up correctly and later used correctly.

The final parameter error free function was assessed through a demonstration of the teams, a cursory code review, and the presence of tests and their traceability to requirements.

No formal audit was defined concerning security. The assessment of secure coding standards was guided by the documents of the Open Web Application Security Project [18]. The two experts audited the submitted projects for possible injection attacks and sufficient logging and monitoring, as well as security configuration. However, ensuring security of the system and verifying that security goals have been met was outside of the scope of the assessment.

5   Results

Five agile software development teams (team A, B, C, D and E) that fulfilled predefined technical requirements were invited to take part in one day workshops. Reykjavik City wanted to assess both how the teams performed during the workshops and the quality of the deliverables they handed in. The three performance factors were: (1) team collaboration and user experience (UX) focus, (2) user stories delivery and (3) the quality of the code. The performance factors were assessed by four experts, two experts assessed the team collaboration and UX focus during the workshops, and two experts assessed the user stories delivery and the quality of the code after the workshops by reviewing the deliverables. The results from the assessment of the performance factors are shown in Table 1.

Team A got the highest number of points in total for the three performance factors. This team had an interesting approach. They only focused on one user story, which was

Table 1. The total points that each team received for the three performance factors evaluated

Performance factor	Team A	Team B	Team C	Team D	Team E
Team collaboration and UX focus *max 25 points*	**25,0**	12,4	9,4	7,6	19,4
Delivery of user stories *max 10 points*	3,3	6,7	6,7	**10,0**	6,7
Quality of code *max 35 points*	22,0	16,2	18,0	**22,4**	**22,4**
Total *max 70 points*	**50,3**	**35,3**	**34,1**	**40,0**	**48,5**

user story 1, during the workshop, but all the other teams selected more than one user story to focus on. This is why Team A got the lowest number of points for the user stories delivered. The user story that Team A selected was the only story that included the citizens of Reykjavik, the other three user stories included employees of Reykjavik city.

Team A got the highest number possible for team collaboration and UX focus. This was the only team that contacted a domain expert to understand the needs of this particular group of citizens. They called a person at the service center and interviewed her/him to enhance their understanding of the needs of the user group. One of the team members also went to the service center, which was in the same building, and tried out how the application process was during the day of the workshop. The other teams did not contact any people outside the team for gathering information on the users and only imaged how the users would behave. These teams got much lower score on the user experience focus sub factor than team A.

The results on the team collaboration factors were more similar for the teams, but still there were some differences. For some teams we did not see much communication during the daily Scrum meeting and the organizing meeting, so the team members did sit by their computers and work individually. This is against the fundamental rules of agile, where team communication and collaboration is vital [16].

The aggregate score for the quality of the code had much less variation in the rating. Teams A, D, and E received almost the same score on code quality. Each of these teams were very competent. The experts observed some differences in each of the 8 categories among these teams but the differences averaged out.

Team B did not document their code and did not trace decisions to requirements and stories. Exceptional behavior was not handled, and no tests were provided. Team C did not document parts of their code well, had many non-descriptive messages like "log in stuff" as commit messages to their version control systems, and did not take care of exceptional code paths. One error message displayed to the user was: "An unexpected error happened" and some errors were silently ignored. They aimed to implement three of the four stories, but only managed to finish two of them. Team D worked on a technical level, planning to implement all the user stories with a high standard of quality. At the same time, they chose the simplest stories. Team D and E received the same scores on code quality but aspects of code quality differed, e.g., team E had worse documentation of their process and the code, but handled web accessibility, error handling, and software architecture better than Team D.

To summarize the findings, it was surprising for all the experts how much variation there was in how the teams worked and what they delivered. All the teams included IT professionals with the technical requirements fulfilled. Team A got the job since they got the highest score of the summary of all the performance factors and their prize estimations were in line with the other teams, so they got the highest total score and the job. They were the only team that reached out to understand the users of the service, while focusing on the code quality in parallel.

6 Lessons Learned

In this section we will summarize the lessons learned for taking part in the assessment of these performance factors.

For assessing the performance of the teams during the workshops it was essential to have the questions behind each sub factor to decide what to focus on during the assessment. Some of the sub factors were harder to assess than others. The sub factor on how the planning meeting for the day was conducted was rather straight forward to assess, since there are procedures on how a good meeting should be conducted from the literature. The experts observed, for example: if all team members were active, if it was clear who was doing what and if they prioritized the user stories. The sub factor on how problem solving oriented the team was, was maybe the hardest to assess, since there is not one activity or time frame, where this should happen. This is more like an assessment of the underlying values in the team and is therefore harder to assess.

For planning the assessment there were a lot of work done on deciding and describing the assessment criteria. This is vital in such work. A recommendation to readers that would want to conduct a similar process is to plan the assessment well and focus on issues that are valuable, but rather straight forward to assess.

Some of the technical measurements had little impact on the overall assessment. For example, the experts concluded that the commit messages had no impact on the total result. This is certainly a result of the workshop format. The experts looked at the commit messages that the teams generated during the day. Four out of five teams focused on implementing as many story points as possible. Therefore, the experts have observed the same poor quality of comments and gave the same grade. The second recommendation to readers is not to assess this factor using the work of a single day.

The quality of web accessibility was assessed. The experts concluded that this score was mostly determined by the choice of the web framework used by each team. The experts observed that little was done to provide accessibility beyond what the framework provided. In this particular project many of the users of the web solution have special needs. For this reason, we recommend to include and emphasize user stories that involve users with special needs when planning such workshops, e.g. a visually impaired user or a colorblind user. The experts commented that while this may make the teams display skills in web accessibility, this comes with the caveat that the assessment may include the same factor twice: as a technical score and as part of the story points' delivery.

Error handling in the interface was not a priority of the teams during the day either. This was surprising to the experts. Input validation was not consistently performed, and invalid inputs were too often reported in obscure ways or not at all. Cryptic error messages in English (not the language of the interface) and stack traces were displayed too often. While the experts gave low scores for this factor, they cannot recommend to ignore this.

The technical factors that had biggest impact on the selection of the agile team were the documentation in the code and error handling in code. The experts could observe that the teams that attempted to document their architecture, the activities their system performed, and that tried to trace code to requirements produced better code. Those teams also tended to handle errors well in code, typically by logging the error and displaying an error message. Again, care has to be taken to not account a deficiency twice. The experts graded an error handled well in code even if the result was a stack trace displayed in the user interface.

A summary of the recommendations includes:

- The planning of the assessment should be done thoroughly and carefully, keeping in mind the values that the agile team should focus on during the actual project. In this particular project many of the users of the web solution have special needs. Therefore one of the sub factors assessed was the emphasis of the teams on user experience during the workshops.
- Meaningful stories should be provided to the teams that involve users with special needs. For these users the focus on accessibility and user experience is very important. Assessing the teams focus on these quality factors is vital in these cases. If the teams do not focus on the quality aspects for these users they are not likely to focus on these aspects for other users.
- If the work of a single day workshop is assessed, the assessment should include the focus on the documentation and how it manages to trace code to requirements,
- The assessment should include to check how the application handles exceptional cases and how it provides feedback to the user in exceptional cases.

References

1. Baggem, R., Correia, J.P., Schill, K., Visser, J.: Standardized code quality benchmarking for improving software maintainability. Software Qual. J. **20**(2), 287–307 (2012). https://doi.org/10.1007/s11219-011-9144-9
2. Billestrup, J., Stage, J., Larusdottir, M.: A case study of four IT companies developing usable public digital self-service solutions. In: The Ninth International Conference on Advances in Computer-Human Interactions (2016)
3. Caldwell, B., Cooper, M., Guarino Reid, L., Vanderheiden, G.: Web Content Accessibility Guidelines (WCAG) 2.0. W3C (2008)
4. Cohn, M.: User Stories Applied. O'Reilly Media, Sebastopol (2004)
5. Curtis, B., Dickenson, B., Kinsey, C.: CISQ Recommendation Guide (2015). https://www.it-cisq.org/adm-sla/CISQ-Rec-Guide-Effective-Software-Quality-Metrics-for-ADM-Service-Level-Agreements.pdf. Accessed 27 June 2019

6. Directive (EU) 2016/2102 of the European Parliament: Directive (EU) 2016/2102 of the European Parliament and of the Council of 26 October 2016 on the accessibility of the websites and mobile applications of public sector bodies (Text with EEA relevance). http://data.europa.eu/eli/dir/2016/2102/oj. Accessed 27 June 2019

7. European Telecommunications Standards Institute: Accessibility requirements suitable for public procurement of ICT products and services in Europe, EN 301 549 V1.1.2 (2015). https://www.etsi.org/deliver/etsi_en/301500_301599/301549/01.01.02_60/en_301549v010102p.pdf

8. Hassenzahl, M.: User experience and experience design. In: Soegaard, M., Dam, R.F. (eds.) The Encyclopedia of Human–Computer Interaction, 2nd edn. The Interaction Design Foundation, Århus (2013)

9. Heitlager, I., Kuipers, T., Visser, J.: A practical model for measuring maintainability. In: 6th International Conference on the Quality of Information and Communications Technology (QUATIC 2007), pp. 30–39. IEEE Computer Society (2007)

10. International organisation for standardisation: ISO 9241-210: 2010. Ergonomics of human-system interaction - Part 210: Human-centred design process for interactive systems (2010)

11. Jia, Y., Larusdottir, M.K., Cajander, Å.: The usage of usability techniques in scrum projects. In: Winckler, M., Forbrig, P., Bernhaupt, R. (eds.) HCSE 2012. LNCS, vol. 7623, pp. 331–341. Springer, Heidelberg (2012). https://doi.org/10.1007/978-3-642-34347-6_25

12. Jokela, T., Laine, J., Nieminen, M.: Usability in RFP's: the current practice and outline for the future. In: Kurosu, M. (ed.) HCI 2013. LNCS, vol. 8005, pp. 101–106. Springer, Heidelberg (2013). https://doi.org/10.1007/978-3-642-39262-7_12

13. Kelly, B., Sloan, D., Phipps, L., Petrie, H., Hamilton, F.: Forcing standardization or accommodating diversity?: A framework for applying the WCAG in the real world. In: Proceedings of the 2005 International Cross-Disciplinary Workshop on Web Accessibility (W4A), pp. 46–54. ACM (2005). https://doi.org/10.1145/1061811.1061820

14. Lallemand, C., Guillaume, G., Vincent, K.: User experience: a concept without consensus? Exploring practitioners' perspectives through an international survey. Comput. Hum. Behav. **43**, 35–48 (2015)

15. Law, E.L., Lárusdóttir, M.K.: Whose experience do we care about? Analysis of the fitness of Scrum and Kanban to user experience. International Journal of Human-Computer Interaction **31**(9), 584–602 (2015)

16. Manifesto for Agile Software Development homepage. https://agilemanifesto.org/. Accessed 27 June 2019

17. Ohno, T.: The Toyota Production System: Beyond Large-Scale Production. Productivity Press, Portland (1988)

18. OWASP Homepage, https://www.owasp.org, last accessed 27th June, 2019

19. Preece, J., Rogers, Y., Sharp, H.: Interaction Design: Beyond Human-Computer Interaction, 5th edn. Wiley, New York (2019)

20. Sjøberg, D.I.K.: The relationship between software process, context and outcome. In: Abrahamsson, P., Jedlitschka, A., Nguyen Duc, A., Felderer, M., Amasaki, S., Mikkonen, T. (eds.) PROFES 2016. LNCS, vol. 10027, pp. 3–11. Springer, Cham (2016). https://doi.org/10.1007/978-3-319-49094-6_1

21. Schwaber, K.: Scrum development process. In: SIGPLAN Notices, vol. 30, no. 10 (1995)

22. Tarkkanen, K., Harkke, V.: Evaluation for evaluation: usability work during tendering process. In Proceedings of the 33rd Annual ACM Conference Extended Abstracts on Human Factors in Computing Systems (CHI EA 2015), pp. 2289–2294. ACM, New York (2015). https://doi.org/10.1145/2702613.2732851

23. Version One: 13th Annual State of Agile survey (2019). https://www.stateofagile.com/#ufh-i-521251909-13th-annual-state-of-agile-report/473508. Accessed 27 June 2019

Characterizing Sets of Systems: Representation and Analysis of Across-Systems Properties

Elodie Bouzekri[1]([✉]) [iD], Alexandre Canny[1] [iD], Célia Martinie[1] [iD],
and Philippe Palanque[1,2] [iD]

[1] ICS-IRIT, Toulouse University, Toulouse, France
{elodie.bouzekri,alexandre.canny,celia.martinie,
philippe.palanque}@irit.fr
[2] Department of Industrial Design, Eindhoven University of Technology,
Eindhoven, The Netherlands

Abstract. System quality is assessed with respect to the value of relevant properties of that system. The level of abstraction of these properties can be very high (e.g. usability) or very low (e.g. all the "Ok" buttons in the application have the same size). These properties can be generic and thus applicable to a large group of systems (e.g. all the interactive systems should be usable) or very specific to a system (e.g. the "Quit" button in my application should always be visible). While properties identification and verification is at the core of interactive systems engineering, much less attention is paid to properties that aims at characterizing a pair (or more) of systems. In this paper, we propose to study such properties (defined as *across-systems* properties) and propose a notation for representing them. We propose a process for the analysis of such properties using the proposed notation. This process and analysis can be used during systems design or integration. We also present several examples of *across-systems* properties and demonstrate their importance and use on a simple example of aircraft cockpits buttons.

Keywords: Properties · Within-system properties · Across-systems properties · Interactive systems · Notation · Aircraft cockpits

1 Introduction

The term property conveys multiple meanings in different domains. However, in computing systems domain [18], they are used to describe characteristics that the system should exhibit but their assessment (on a given system) is usually a complex and cumbersome activity. Formal description techniques are aimed at describing both the system and their expected properties and to demonstrate (or not) that the system really exhibits these properties.

Figure 1 presents the process advocated by DO178-C standard [22] for the design of computing systems in the aeronautics domain. That process highlights the need for explicit representation of expected properties for a given aircraft system (bottom of the Figure) and the formal methods supplement to this standard [17] even recommend the

© IFIP International Federation for Information Processing 2020
Published by Springer Nature Switzerland AG 2020
J. Abdelnour Nocera et al. (Eds.): INTERACT 2019, LNCS 11930, pp. 84–96, 2020.
https://doi.org/10.1007/978-3-030-46540-7_9

use of CTL (Computational Tree Logic) from [21] to represent them. The right-hand side of the Figure highlights the activity of formal verification that checks whether properties hold on the behavioral description of the system produced in the LLR phase (upper part of the Figure). Such approach follows the work done by Sistla and Pnueli [19] on the safety and liveness properties of reactive systems. Their focus, and the one of DO 330 standard, is on the representation of multiple properties for a single system under design or evaluation.

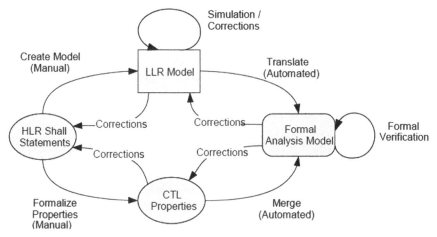

Fig. 1. Formal Approach to System Design as in DO178C– Supplement 330 on Formal Methods [17]

The HCI community usually focusses on properties that characterize a single system in relation to the user and his/her environment. For instance, the well-studied usability property determines the effectiveness, the efficiency and the satisfaction according to standard ISO 9241 [7] of the system for a given user (or set of users). Other usability definitions add learnability [12] or accessibility [14] to the standard definition. Usability evaluation can be performed on one single system. In other words, the usability evaluation function needs one parameter (a system) and returns a set of value. This means that for usability evaluation would blend a value for the effectiveness of the system, a value for the efficiency of the system and one for the satisfaction of the user using the system. One important aspect of this is that the type of the values depends on the property. It can be Boolean (the property is true or false) but also enumerated type or a number (e.g. error rate). We call *within-system* property this kind of property for which the evaluation function needs one single system as parameter. User Experience [15], privacy [5], dependability and security [2] are other examples of *within-system* properties that can be evaluated on a single system. In contrast, other systems properties can be evaluated only with, at least, two systems as parameter. For instance, similarity property determines the distance between several interfaces in terms of orientation, order and density of their items (according to the definition in [6]). The evaluation function of similarity needs at least two parameters (two user interfaces) and returns a set of three values: one for the orientation, one for the order and one for the density. We call this kind of properties *across-systems* properties. Proximity [16] and congruence [3] are other examples of *across-systems* properties, as their evaluation function needs at least two parameters too. Less attention is paid to *across-systems* properties even though these properties can be extremely useful to characterize sets of systems as, for instance, in the prototyping phases of interactive systems development where multiple alternatives are designed and assessed. We propose to investigate and define different *across-systems* properties and a mean to describe explicitly these properties in interactive systems design process.

In the next section, we detail different examples of *across-systems* properties. In the third section, we propose QSCA notation supported by the DREAMER tool to represent *across-systems* properties. In the fourth section, we propose a process for the analysis of *across-systems* properties of systems using QSCA notation. The fifth section illustrates how this notation and process help in describing the *across-systems* properties of aircraft cockpit elements. Section 5 concludes the paper and highlights directions for future work.

2   Examples of Existing Across-Systems Properties

Across-systems properties are meant to characterize the quality of a set of systems. As mentioned in the introduction, Similarity is an *across-systems* property that aims at assessing the distance between the visual layouts of several systems interfaces in terms of orientation, order and density as introduced in [6], refined in [11] and more recently used for experience gathering [23]. This Similarity property can be included as a contributing factor of the Proximity property. The term Proximity is used by Wickens and Carswell [16] as compatibility principle between sets of displays for interface design. We propose to use the term Proximity as defined in [16] to be an *across-systems* property. The Proximity *across-systems* property is composed of Perceptual Proximity and Processing Proximity [16]. Perceptual proximity includes:

- the spatial proximity of displayed items,
- the visual connection between displayed items,
- the similarity (e.g. color, orientation) between displayed items,
- the homogeneous information display (i.e. all digital, all analogous, both),
- the object integration (i.e. contiguity, contour and spatial integration) of displayed items.

   Processing proximity includes:

- the cognitive processing proximity of the tasks,
- the similarity between units of the displayed parameters,
- the temporal proximity of the task (i.e. the time to perform the task).

Another example of *across-systems* property is Congruence. Dekker and Hollnagel [3] define Congruence as the ability of the system to take into account the variation of user capabilities and needs depending on the current situation. Extending this proposal, we propose to consider congruence across a set of systems. In other words, Congruence property aims at characterizing the ability of a set of systems to maintain their input/output compatible with user capabilities and needs whatever the situation.

Finally, we propose a list of *across-systems* properties that are initially within-system properties but that can also be applied as *across-systems* properties:

- Equivalency: One or several systems exhibit the same properties as another system or several systems.
- Dependency: One or several systems depend on the outputs of other systems. For instance, a set of radio receptors are dependent from a radio transmitter, as receptors need the radio waves of the transmitter.
- Complementarity: Each system belonging to a set of systems performs a share of the overall activity. The complete work is the union of each part. For instance, a set of factory robots of production line highly support complementary property, as each robot completes the work produced by the previous one.
- Diversity: Each system of the set of systems is implemented in a different language or technology. A set composed of a C++ application, a JAVA application and a Python application highly supports diversity property [24].
- Redundancy: Each system of the set of systems offers the same functions. For instance, a set composed of a computer extinguisher application and an extinguisher physical button of the computer highly support redundancy property for the shutdown function [26].
- Equality: The control authority is equally distributed between the systems of the set. For instance, a set of systems under the so-called "master-slave" protocol have a very low equality property.
- Uniformity: Each system of the set contributes with the same amount of work to the overall activity.
- Concurrency: Each system of the set of systems work at the same time [25].

Defining properties of set of systems is useful to analyze how to integrate several systems for a particular function or to replace a system by another one inside an integrated set of systems. For example, in aircrafts, to integrate a system as a backup in case of a failure of another system, redundancy and diversity are important properties (that are related to the implementation of fault tolerance mechanisms [2, 4]). Another example is the replacement of a system by a newest one in a factory. In order to minimize the learning time for the operators, the proximity property has to be assessed (to ensure that the required number of new cognitive tasks to learn is low). In the same way that *within-system* properties may be used to define requirements for the systems and then drive the design of these systems, *across-systems* properties also may be targeted during the design of an integrated set of systems. In order to provide support for the comparison of design options with respect to a set of *across-systems* properties, we propose to extend TEAM design rationale notation (which is based on QOC [9]).

3   QSCA Notation: Extensions to the QOC and TEAM Notations

MacLean et al. [9] introduced the QOC (Question Option Criteria) notation for system design rational. QOC allows to document design choices with their explanations during the design process. This notation is also a tool for reasoning and communicating with various stakeholders as it uses very simple concepts. The TEAM (Traceability, Exploration and Analysis Method) [10] notation extends the QOC notation with the description of properties and factors associated to the criteria, as well as with the identification of design artefacts associated to the design options.

We propose to extend the TEAM notation to enable the representation of *across-systems* properties, in order to take into account across-systems properties when designing a set of systems. For that purpose, we propose to slightly adapt the TEAM notation to create QSCA notation:

- Question: Design question about the system under design (Square in Fig. 2).
- System: possible option for the system to answer the design question (Disc in Fig. 2) replaces design option of the TEAM notation.
- Concrete property: Desired property met (or not) by the related set of systems (Lower right triangle in Fig. 2) replaces the desired property met by one or several design options of TEAM notation.
- *Across-systems* property (Upper right triangle in Fig. 2) encompassing the concrete property of several systems. If a system option highly supports an across-systems property, a plain line is drawn between this *across-systems* property and the line that connect a system option and the concrete property associated to this across-systems property. If a system option gives few support to an across-systems property, a dashed line is drawn between this *across-systems* property and the line that connect a system option and the concrete property associated to this across-systems property. *Across-systems* property replaces the notation element *Argument* of the TEAM notation. The notation element *Argument* stands for the reason behind the choice of one design option in the TEAM notation.

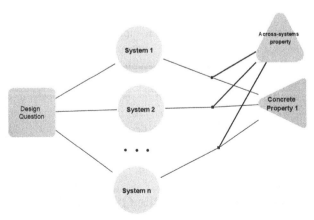

Fig. 2. Main elements of the QSCA notation (extension to the notation TEAM) edited with the DREAMER tool

The DREAMER (Design Rationale Environment for Argumentation and Modeling and Engineering Requirements) tool supports recording, edition and analysis of TEAM models [10]. We propose to use DREAMER to describe QSCA models.

4   From the *Across-Systems* Properties Description to a Process for the Analysis of *Across-Systems* Properties of Systems

In this section, we present the process for the analysis of *across-systems* properties of systems. This process presented in Fig. 3 can be used for various purposes during the design process (e.g. design choices or integration of systems).

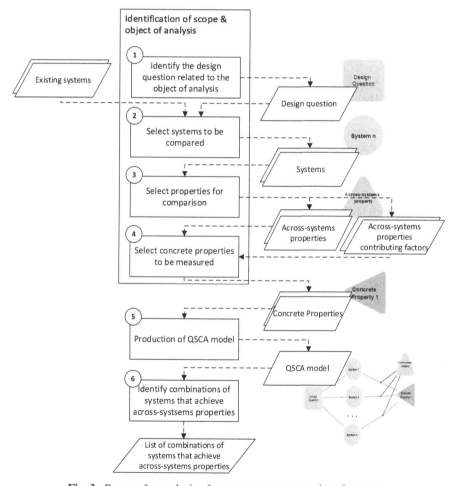

Fig. 3. Process for analysis of *across-systems* properties of systems.

During the first step, the involved stakeholders identify the design question related to the object of the analysis. For example, a design question can be "what are the most similar systems?". They describe this design question in the QSCA model. During the step 2, they select the systems to compare. They describe these systems in the QSCA model. During the step 3, they identify the *across-systems* properties they want the selected systems to support. They identify the contributing factors of the selected *across-systems* properties as well. In the same way as the selection of *within-system* properties, the selection of *across-systems* properties can result from user studies, organizational or legal constraints. As for *within-systems* properties, it is possible that only some of the contributing factors of the *across-systems* property are identified relevant to support. For example, the appearance and identification contributing factors of UX *within-system* property can be identified relevant to the detriment of others during a user study. In the same way, the similarity of users tasks contributing factor of Proximity *across-systems* property can be identified relevant to the detriment of the others contributing factors. They describe the selected *across-systems* properties and/or *across-systems* property contributing factors in the QSCA model. During the step 4, they select the concrete properties to be measured on selected systems. For example, a concrete property of Similarity *across-systems* property is "same interface items orientation". They describe these concrete properties in the QSCA model. During the step 5, they produce the final QSCA model. They describe how (strongly denied, denied, neutral, supported, strongly supported) the combinations of systems support each concrete property in the QSCA model and how these concrete properties support their relative *across-systems* properties. During step 6, they identify the combinations of systems that achieve *across-systems* properties. As a result, at the end of the process, the list of combinations of systems that achieve the *across-systems* properties is identified.

For the illustrative example of this paper, we follow this process and use the DREAMER tool [10] to analyze *across-systems* properties of different system designs of the FIRE push-button in an aircraft cockpit.

5   Representing Across-Systems Properties: Illustrative Example

In the A350 aircraft cockpit, there are guarded FIRE push-buttons on the overhead panel, one for each engine of the aircraft. These buttons are composed of a backlighting system, a guard and a toggle button (see Fig. 4). When a fire is detected in an engine, the backlighting system turns on and the pilot must raise the guard and press the toggle button [1] to acknowledge the alarm. When the button is pressed, all the systems that are connected to the engine are isolated and the fire extinguisher bottles are armed for a possible discharge [1].

In this example, we study the digitalization of such FIRE push-button (FIRE pb). Two different designs of the digital FIRE pb are proposed.

The first design option mimics all the graphical aspects and interactions of the physical FIRE pb. The difference is that the button is no more physical and user interactions must be performed with a mouse. The sequence of interaction is visible in Fig. 5. Like the physical FIRE pb, the user sees the backlighting system on, raises the guard and presses the button to isolate the engine and to prepare the bottles to discharge. We call this design option "overhead panel-like FIRE pb".

Fig. 4. Engine 1 FIRE push-button on the overhead panel.

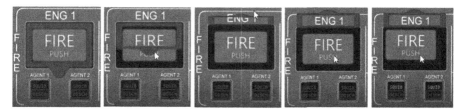

Fig. 5. Interactions sequence for pushing overhead panel-like FIRE push button

The second design option supports a different interaction sequence that still enables the guard of the button. This interaction sequence is similar to the GoPro[1] unlock inter-action and is called GoPro-like FIRE pb. This sequence of interactions is presented in Fig. 6 and is composed of the following steps: the user sees the backlighting system on, drags the button on the bolt area, maintains the button in this area until the anima-tion finishes, releases and presses the button to isolate engine and prepare the bottles to discharge. For this proposed interaction design, the attention has been paid to respect the same interaction time to remove the guard and press the button as with the physical FIRE pb.

We propose to analyze these different designs with the physical FIRE pb with respect to a subset of the *across-systems* properties presented in Sect. 2 in order to choose a digital design for the FIRE push-button. This goal is described by "which user control to perform an acknowledgment of fire?" design question (step 1 of the process described in Fig. 3). The systems to be compared are the physical, the overhead panel-like and GoPro-like fire push-buttons (step 2 of the process).

For this illustrative example, we choose to compare the push-buttons relative to their processing proximity, homogeneous information display, temporal proximity (contribut-ing factors of Proximity *across-systems* property), redundancy and similarity (*across-systems* properties) (step 3 of the process). We choose "same graphical rendering", "same functions", "same time to perform tasks", "same logical processing", and the type of the output (physical and digital) as concrete properties to be measured on push-buttons

---

[1] https://gopro.com.

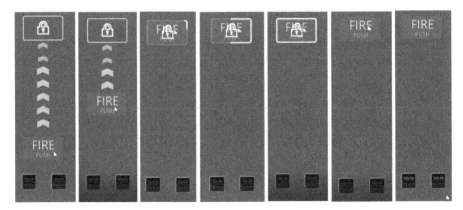

Fig. 6. Interactions sequence for pushing GoPro-like FIRE push-button

(step 4). We describe in the QSCA model (Fig. 7) how the combinations of push-buttons support or not the concrete properties (step 5). The actual FIRE pb and overhead panel-like FIRE pb have the same graphical rendering. Then, they support the Similarity *across-systems* property (first multi-systems property from the bottom of Fig. 7) (step 6). All the systems have the same functions: fire alert, isolate engine and prepare the fire extinguisher bottles to discharge. Then, these systems support the Redundancy *across-systems* property (second multi-systems property from the bottom of Fig. 7) (step 6). All the systems are designed so that it takes the same time to perform the button push. Then, they support the temporal proximity *across-systems* property (step 6). The physical FIRE pb is physical whereas overhead panel-like and GoPro-like FIRE pb are digital. Then, they provide low support to the homogeneous information display *across-systems* property (step 6). Finally, all systems require the same logical processing user task: the button can be pushed to prepare fire extinguishing when the backlighting system is on and guard raised. Then, all the systems support the processing proximity *across-systems* property (step 6).

Across-systems properties can inform the design option decision if a single digital option must be chosen. In order to not modify the pilot training procedure as applied with the current physical FIRE pb, the preferred option should be the overhead panel-like FIRE pb one. Indeed, all of the design options are graphically alike and user cognitive tasks are close (similarity and processing proximity). Otherwise, despite the use of different input devices and interactions techniques used for the three design options, their *across-systems* properties indicate that they are alike. In this case, usability evaluation can be performed to discriminate the most suitable option according to the users.

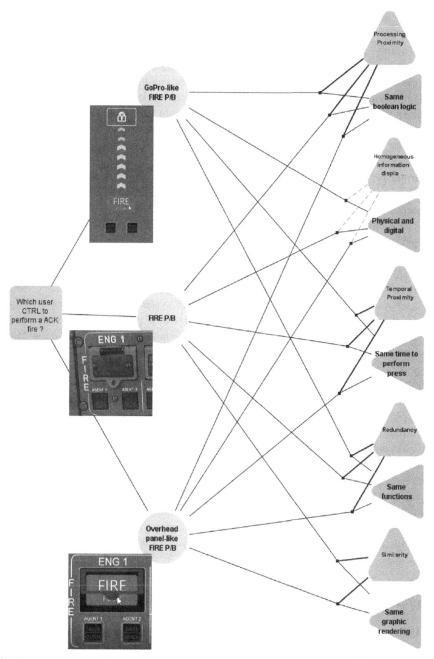

Fig. 7. Representation of *across-systems* properties of FIRE pb, GoPro-like FIRE pb and overhead panel-like FIRE pb using extended QOC & TEAM notations to answer the design question "Which user control to perform *acknowledge fire* action?"

6 Conclusion

This position paper introduces the concept of *across-systems* properties and proposes a mean to represent *across-systems* properties using QSCA notation based on TEAM and a process. It illustrates (on an example) how one can use it. This example is based on the physical FIRE push-button found in an aircraft cockpit and on its digital design alternatives (if we consider that future cockpits would replace such physical buttons with touch screen interactions). Even though, the physical FIRE push-button and digital alternatives seem to be very different, *across-systems* properties highlights their common characteristics and suitability to pilot tasks. In addition, if designers want to replace the current system by a digital one or want to integrate a redundant one, the representation of *across-systems* properties can guide design choices depending on the properties designers want to preserve and the ones they are ready to abandon.

In the same way as the pilot does not only use the FIRE push-button to deal with an engine fire (they could do testing for instance), it is common for users to manipulate several systems to reach a goal. In other words, users can use complex systems composed of several sub-systems to perform their work. For instance, an office employee use several systems such as a computer, a telephone and a printer to perform his/her work. All these systems compose a workstation complex system. For this reason, it might be interesting to investigate possible links between *within-system* properties of systems and *across-system* properties of the entire work environment. For instance, redundancy *across-system* property is also a fault tolerant technique to contribute to the *within-system* dependability [2] of a given system. Looking at each redundant component, we might want to identify *within-system* properties (e.g. performance). The variants used for redundancy must exhibit similar behaviors and thus similarity is, for them, an across-system property. If similarity is guaranteed then the fault-tolerant system embedding all the redundant ones will exhibit dependability as a *within-system* property.

One perspective to this work lays in the analysis of how *within-system* properties can help designers when they have to integrate several systems. For example, if several systems of the cockpit have a high proximity, the integration of these systems to support a user goal may enhance the usability of the whole cockpit, as pointed out by Huchins in the work on distributed cognition [27]. In other words, the description of the relationship between *within-system* properties and *across-system* properties can enable to understand how the first influences the second and to design systems with a more global integrated perspective.

References

1. Airbus A350 Flight Crew Operating Manual, 5T1 A350 FLEET FCOM. Technical Report. Airbus
2. Avizienis, A., Laprie, J.C., Randell, B., Landwehr, C.: Basic concepts and taxonomy of dependable and secure computing. IEEE Trans. Depend. Secure Comput. **1**, 11–33 (2004). https://doi.org/10.1109/TDSC.2004.2
3. Dekker, S., Hollnagel, E.: Coping with Computers in the Cockpit. Routledge, Abingdon (2018)

4. Fayollas, C., Martinie, C., Navarre, D., Palanque, P., Fahssi, R.: Fault-tolerant user interfaces for critical systems: duplication, redundancy and diversity as new dimensions of distributed user interfaces. In: Proceedings of the 2014 Workshop on Distributed User Interfaces and Multimodal Interaction, pp. 27–30. ACM, New York (2014). https://doi.org/10.1145/2677356.2677662

5. Gerber, P., Volkamer, M., Renaud, K.: Usability versus privacy instead of usable privacy: Google's balancing act between usability and privacy. SIGCAS Comput. Soc. **45**, 16–21 (2015). https://doi.org/10.1145/2738210.2738214

6. Heil, S., Bakaev, M., Gaedke, M.: Measuring and ensuring similarity of user interfaces: the impact of web layout. In: Cellary, W., Mokbel, M.F., Wang, J., Wang, H., Zhou, R., Zhang, Y. (eds.) WISE 2016. LNCS, vol. 10041, pp. 252–260. Springer, Cham (2016). https://doi.org/10.1007/978-3-319-48740-3_18

7. International Standard Organization: "ISO 9241-11" Ergonomic requirements for office work with visual display terminals (VDT) – Part 11 Guidance on Usability (1996)

8. Lazar, J., Feng, J.H., Hochheiser, H.: Research Methods in Human-Computer Interaction. Morgan Kaufmann, Burlington (2017)

9. MacLean, A., Young, R.M., Bellotti, V.M.E., Moran, T.P.: Questions, Options, and Criteria: Elements of Design Space Analysis. Human-Computer Interaction. **6**, 201–250 (1991). https://doi.org/10.1080/07370024.1991.9667168

10. Martinie, C., Palanque, P., Winckler, M., Conversy, S.: DREAMER: a design rationale environment for argumentation, modeling and engineering requirements. In: Proceedings of the 28th ACM International Conference on Design of Communication. pp. 73–80. ACM, New York (2010). https://doi.org/10.1145/1878450.1878463

11. Navarre, D., Palanque, P., Hamon, A., Della Pasqua, S.: Similarity as a design driver for user interfaces of dependable critical systems. In: Clemmensen, T., Rajamanickam, V., Dannenmann, P., Petrie, H., Winckler, M. (eds.) INTERACT 2017. LNCS, vol. 10774, pp. 114–122. Springer, Cham (2018). https://doi.org/10.1007/978-3-319-92081-8_11

12. Nielsen, J.: Usability Engineering. Elsevier, Amsterdam (1994)

13. Oxford Dictionary. https://en.oxforddictionaries.com/definition/property

14. Petrie, H., Kheir, O.: The relationship between accessibility and usability of websites. In: Proceedings of the SIGCHI Conference on Human Factors in Computing Systems. pp. 397–406. ACM, New York (2007).

15. Pirker, M.M., Bernhaupt, R.: Measuring user experience in the living room: results from an ethnographically oriented field study indicating major evaluation factors. In: Proceedings of the 9th European Conference on Interactive TV and Video, pp. 79–82. ACM, New York (2011)

16. Wickens, C.D., Carswell, C.M.: The proximity compatibility principle: its psychological foundation and relevance to display design. Hum. Factors: J. Hum. Factors Ergon. Soc. **37**, 473–494 (1995)

17. DO-333 Formal Methods Supplement to DO-178C and DO-278A, published by RTCA and EUROCAE, 13 December 2011

18. Manna, Z., Pnueli, A.: A hierarchy of temporal properties. ACM Symp. Principles Distrib. Comput. **1990**, 377–410 (1990)

19. Sistla, A.P.: On characterization of safety and liveness properties in temporal logic. In: Proceedings of the Fourth Annual ACM Symposium on Principles of Distributed Computing, pp. 39–48. ACM (1985)

20. Pnueli, A.: Applications of temporal logic to the specification and verification of reactive systems: a survey of current trends. In: de Bakker, J.W., de Roever, W.-P., Rozenberg, G. (eds.) Current Trends in Concurrency. LNCS, vol. 224, pp. 510–584. Springer, Heidelberg (1986). https://doi.org/10.1007/BFb0027047

21. Clarke, E., Emerson, E.A.: Design and synthesis of synchronization skeletons using branching time temporal logic. In: Logic of Programs: Workshop, Yorktown Heights, NY, May 1981, vol. 131 (1981)
22. DO-178C/ED-12C, Software Considerations in Airborne Systems and Equipment Certification, published by RTCA and EUROCAE (2012)
23. Zhao, X., Littlewood, B., Povyakalo, A.A., Strigini, L., Wright, D.: Conservative claims for the probability of perfection of a software-based system using operational experience of previous similar systems. Reliab. Eng. Syst. Saf. **175**, 265–282 (2018)
24. Gashi, I., Povyakalo, A., Strigini, L.: Diversity, Safety and Security in Embedded Systems: Modelling Adversary Effort and Supply Chain Risks. EDCC 2016, pp. 13–24 (2016)
25. Best, E.: Semantics of Sequential and Parallel Programs. Prentice Hall International series in computer science, Prentice Hall, pp. I-XI, pp. 1–351 (1996), ISBN 978-0-13-460643-9
26. Avizienis, A.: The Methodology of N-version Programming. In: Lyu, M. (ed.) Software Fault Tolerance. Wiley, Hoboken (1995)
27. Hollan, J., Hutchins, E., Kirsh, D.: Distributed cognition: toward a new foundation for human-computer interaction research. ACM Trans. Comput. Hum. Interact. **7**(2), 174–196 (2000)

Designing an Intelligent User Interface for Preventing Phishing Attacks

Joseph Aneke[1] (ID), Carmelo Ardito[2](✉) (ID), and Giuseppe Desolda[1] (ID)

[1] Università degli Studi di Bari Aldo Moro, Via Orabona 4, 70125 Bari, Italy
{joseph.aneke,giuseppe.desolda}@uniba.it
[2] Politecnico di Bari, Via Orabona 4, 70125 Bari, Italy
carmelo.ardito@poliba.it

Abstract. Most phishing sites are simply copies of real sites with slight features distorted or in some cases masqueraded. This property of phishing sites has made them difficult for humans and various anti-phishing techniques to detect. Also, the attacker community has proved itself able to quickly adapt to anti-phishing measures, mainly warning messages to help limit the effectiveness of phishing attacks and protect unsuspecting users. Despite the notable advances made in the last years by the active warning messages for phishing, this attack remains one of the most effective. In this paper we propose an intelligent warning message mechanism, that might limit the effectiveness of phishing attacks and that might increase the user awareness about related risks. It implements an intelligent behavior that, besides warning the users that a phishing attack is occurring, explains why the specific suspect site can be fraudulent.

Keywords: Usable security · Intelligent user interfaces · Cybersecurity

1 Introduction

Phishing is a form of social engineering in which an attacker attempts to fraudulently acquire sensitive information from a victim by impersonating a trustworthy third party [1]. Today these attacks typically employ generalized "lures." For instance, a common phishing attack is (for a phisher) to obtain a victim's authentication information corresponding to one website that is mimicked by the attacker and then uses this at another site. This is a successful attack given that many users reuse passwords – whether in verbatim or with only slight changes. This attack is typically carried out by e-mail or instant messaging, and often directs users to enter details at a fake website [2]. A common example is "we need you to confirm your account details or we must shut your account down". The reason why an individual falls prey to this type of trap is that the message, which appears as the victim expects, and therefore legitimate, directs the user to visit fake webpages whose look and feel is similar or identical to the legitimate one. This phishing modality is also known as context-aware attack and is becoming increasingly common. Figure 1 shows an example of a phishing attack sent to a user by email. The email appears genuine from a trusted sender, i.e. "uniba.it" which is the email service

© IFIP International Federation for Information Processing 2020
Published by Springer Nature Switzerland AG 2020
J. Abdelnour Nocera et al. (Eds.): INTERACT 2019, LNCS 11930, pp. 97–106, 2020.
https://doi.org/10.1007/978-3-030-46540-7_10

provider of the user. However, visualizing the details of the sender's identity reveals that it was masquerading to get the user to fill a form.

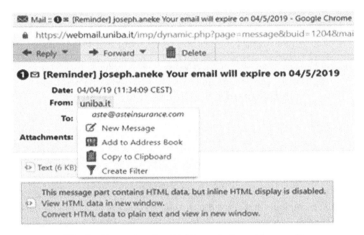

Fig. 1. Example of a phishing attack sent by email.

The effectiveness of phishing techniques, and more in general of cyber-attacks is not only related to the obsolescence of software and hardware. Federal Computer Week reports that almost 59% of security incidents that involve human errors are the result of simple mistakes as opposed to intentional malicious actions [3]. Hosteler found that human error is one of the first cause of cyberattacks (37%) [4]. Furthermore, the simplest and fastest way to start an attack is by means of phishing and social engineering attacks, where 91% of all cyberattacks starts with some kind of phishing email that manipulates users to provide sensitive information via various methods of social engineering [5].

Because of the risks associated with cyberattacks, it is crucial for Internet users to be aware of when they are being attacked and to be successfully informed on how to combat them. The recent demography results by Anti-Phishing Working Group 4th quarter report shows that around 45,794 phishing reports have been chronicled [2]. There is no single way that can prevent all types of phishing. But different methods applied at different stages of a phishing attack can abort the attempt and properly applied technology can significantly reduce the risk of identity theft [6]. Different approaches are already proposed to automatically detect phishing websites [7–9]. These methods and algorithms determine the likelihood that a website can be suspect but without absolute certainty. When the resulting likelihood exceeds a critical threshold, typically the users are informed about the potential risk of phishing attacks. This is done through a visual warning message that should help users in deciding to access or not the suspect website. Despite the significant advances of current warning messages, this attack remains very effective since the users often are not able to make the right decision.

There is a direct need for us to design such a remedy which can address the above problem and stand out from the traditional warning messages available. In this paper, we report on an ongoing work about an intelligent warning message that might limit the effectiveness of phishing attacks and that might increase the user awareness about the related risks. The proposed solution implements an intelligent behavior that explains why the specific suspect site can be fraudulent. It is well-known that explaining the reasons about a fact helps the user being aware of the danger and taking more conscious and adequate decisions [10].

2 Literature Review

Successful security depends on systems, technology and people (including users) collaborating to identify threats, weaknesses, and solutions. However, many initiatives today focus on systems and technology, without addressing well-known user-related issues. In fact, users have been identified as one of the major security weaknesses in today's technologies, as they may be unaware that their behavior while interacting with a system may have security consequences. The user interface is where human users interact with computer systems. It is where the user's intention transforms into the system operation. It is where the semantic gap arises [11]. And this is the aspect that needs more attention to further limit the effectiveness of cyberattacks.

One typical anti-phishing approach is to use visual indicators, for example an informative toolbar, to differentiate legitimate messages from phishing messages [12]. This approach tries to bridge the semantic gap by unveiling to human users the system model and expects them to make a wise decision under phishing attacks. User studies in [13] show that the tested anti-phishing toolbars fail to effectively prevent high-quality phishing attacks. Many subjects failed to constantly pay attention to the toolbar's messages; others disregarded the warnings shown in the toolbar if the web page content looked legitimate. The studies also found that many subjects did not understand phishing attacks or realize how sophisticated such attacks can be.

Emigh provided an overview of several studies regarding phishing and usability of browser security clues [14]. It emerged that phishing is a threat because users are unable to verify the authenticity of a website asking for their credentials. He questioned the ability of users to avoid phishing sites based on security and identification indicators suggesting that the solutions were still inadequate. Varshney et al. proposed Dynamic Security Skins, a browser extension that allows websites to display a secret image and customizes the browser chrome [15]. Anecdotal evidence suggests that some users may still fall victim of those phishing websites which, in order to cheat about their different appearance (e.g., logo not displayed), claim that the image database is down for maintenance or simply do not provide any explanation about this, since logo absence might not trigger users' attention.

In [16], the authors sought to determine if user's education was a possible solution to prevent phishing attacks. They explored the impact of both specific users' characteristics (age, gender, education, knowledge about phishing) and of their Internet usage habits on their ability to correctly identify e-mail messages. Quantitative data was collected by showing to participants e-mail messages and quizzing their ability to correctly categorize them. The results show the variables listed above did influence the participant's ability to correctly identify email messages. Although educational efforts are unlikely to solve the phishing problem on its own, vigilant users form an important part of the defensive strategy. Both research efforts and public education campaigns are still not enough.

A study to determine the impact that communicating to users different security policies has on mitigating phishing attacks is discussed in [9]. The research results reveal that a security policy that contains an explanation of the impact of an attack or a statement indicating an evaluation for non-compliance or a statement from a direct authority provides no significant impact on mitigating phishing attacks [17]. The use of online games to teach users good habits to help them avoid phishing attacks is investigated in [18]. The authors explore the relationship between demographics and phishing susceptibilities, and the effectiveness of several anti-phishing educational materials. Results suggest that women are more susceptible to phishing than men and participants between the ages of 18 and 25 are more likely to be a victim of a phishing attack than other age groups.

A new anti-phishing approach which uses training intervention for phishing web sites detection is discussed in [19]. The results of this work show that technical ability has minimal effect whereas phishing knowledge has a positive effect on phishing web site detection. A system called PhishGuru incorporating an embedded training methodology and learning science principles is proposed in [20]. The Author evaluates the proposed methodology through laboratory and field studies. Results show that people trained with the proposed system retain knowledge even after 28 days. A major drawback is that the system will need to be trained and updated regularly. Robert et al. [21] found that web browser warnings should help protect people from malware, phishing, and network attacks. Adhering to these warnings keeps people safer online. They further demonstrated that recent improvements in warning designs have raised adherence rates, but they could still be higher. And prior work suggests many people still do not understand them. Thus, two challenges remain: increasing both comprehension and adherence rates. The authors in [21] suggested that further improvements to warnings will require solving a range of smaller contextual misunderstandings.

Most phishing sites are simply copies of real sites with the above-mentioned feature slightly distorted or in some cases masqueraded [22]. This property of phishing sites has made them difficult for humans to detect, but fortunately, easier for computers. However, the attacker community has proved itself able to quickly adapt to anti-phishing measures mainly warning messages. Different warning messages have been already evaluated during controlled experiments [21, 23]. Besides evaluating the efficacy of different solutions, these experiments provided useful indications on how to design and evaluate phishing warning messages. Despite the notable advances made in the last years by the active warning messages for phishing [21, 23], this attack remains one the most effective. Indeed, algorithms for detecting phishing attacks are only able to determine the likelihood with which a website can be suspect but without absolute certainty. When the likelihood exceeds a critical threshold the warning messages alert the users about a possible risk and the users have to decide to access or not the website. However, current warning messages have large room for improvement, as shown by the high success rate of phishing attacks reported in [24]. One of the first problems is the click-through effect [25]: the users tend to skip these alerts because they appear always in the same way, thus pushing most users in neglecting these messages. The second problem is the wrong design of the warning messages in term of colors, words, interaction, as underlined by

[21, 23]. Lastly, the users are not experts in cybersecurity, they do not know what a phishing attack is and what are the risks they are exposed to [21].

In order to overcome these limitations, in the following section, we propose an intelligent warning message mechanism that might limit the effectiveness of phishing attacks and that might increase the user awareness about related risks. It implements an intelligent behavior that, besides warning the users that a phishing attack is occurring, explains why the specific suspect site can be fraudulent.

3 A Polymorphic User Interface to Warn Users About Phishing Attacks

An example of polymorphic user interface to warn users about phishing attacks is reported in Fig. 2. In addition to addressing the design guidelines and lesson learned proposed in [21, 23], this prototype shows three panels that explain the reasons why the target website can be a fake. In this example, the first panel specifies that the URL of the target website (www.paypaI.com) looks similar to the original one but the l has been replaced by capital I, thus confusing the users. The second panel reports that the suspect website was created three weeks ago, an age typical of phishing websites. The last box reports information about the HTTPS certificate of the suspect website, explaining that even if the users see safe navigation in the browser toolbar, with a self-signed certificate they are not guaranteed that the site behavior is legitimate.

It is worth remarking that the three panels show different information according to the suspect website, thus different reasons would be reported with different phishing websites. Thank to this intelligent warning message, we address three important goals, i.e.:

1. *Prevent user habituation*: a polymorphic message decreases the clickthrough effect caused by the user habituation [25];
2. *Provide an explanation about the attack*: useful information about the causes of the phishing attacks support the users in deciding if the website is (or not) a phishing attack [26];
3. *Educate the users on cyberattacks and related risks*: a long-term training of the users on phishing attacks is performed since they understand the reasons for this attack [19, 27].

In our work we are not interested to classify phishing websites [7–9]. We start from the assumption that the browser can detect the phishing website through its internal algorithm, or that we use an API to detect malicious sites[1]. Regardless of which of the two solutions we adopt, when a phishing website is detected, instead of displaying the traditional warning messages implemented in the browser, we show the intelligent UI proposed in this paper (see Fig. 2).

To provide users with information that explain the reasons of the phishing attacks, our approach consists of two main steps, i.e., (1) the computation of a set of indicators

---

[1] https://safebrowsing.google.com.

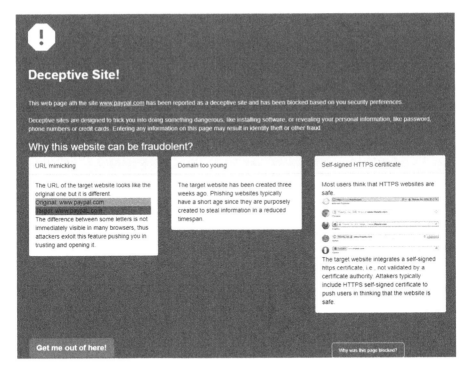

Fig. 2. A prototype of intelligent warning message for phishing attacks.

that can reveal phishing websites and (2) the use of machine learning approaches to select the most important indicators. The three most important indicators will be shown and explained to the user, as shown in the example above.

According to our goal and a literature review [7–9, 28], we are considering indicators for the suspect web sites like:

- *URL*: phishing sites typically have URLs containing more than 2/3 number of digits or "-". In addition, they often try to mimic the original URL changing character that looks similar, for example, "l" with "I";
- *Server location*: phishing websites are often hosted by a web server located in countries where there are no strict laws against cyberattacks;
- *Alexa or search engine rank*: phishing website typically appear after the first 1 million Alexa top results, or in the last positions of search engines like Google Search;
- *Timelife:* this cyber-attack is usually concentrated in a limited time span, thus the suspect website is typically created few days/weeks before the attack;
- *Top-level domain*: attackers typically use free domains to host phishing web sites; one of the most popular is freenom.com, thus domains like ".cf", ".gq", ".ml", ".tk" and ".ga" are common among phishing web sites;
- *Name length:* Attackers may create domains using a specific template, such as random strings of a given length;

- *Archived domain:* a domain archived on the "Wayback Machine" is more likely to be legitimately owned, and vice versa;
- *Self-signed https certificate:* the suspect websites often integrate a self-signed https certificate, i.e., not validated by a certification authority. Including this certificate, attackers confuse users who see safe navigation in the browser toolbar, but without any guarantee about the web site behaviour.

We defined different metrics to calculate each indicator for the suspect website. For example, Alexa rank can be obtained through its API; the Wayback Machine APIs are used to get information about website archiving; SSL certificate is inspected to see if a trustable certification authority signed it. Those indicators, resulting in a numeric value, are normalized in a 0–1 interval using a min-max function, with min and max values obtained calculating each indicator on all the phishing websites available in the *PhishTank* database and selecting for each indicator the min and max value.

After the computation of the indicators, we use a decision tree model to select the most important indicators. In particular, we adopted the C4.5 algorithm to generate our decision tree. This algorithm was developed by Ross Quinlan [29] and it is an extension of Quinlan's earlier ID3 algorithm. The decision trees generated by C4.5 can be used for classification, and in our case to classify the suspect website. However, we are not interested to understand if it is a phishing site, since we already know it. We only exploit this tree to select those three nodes that positively contribute to determining it as phishing. In other words, we use it to filter the indicators that are more influential in the classification process.

After the selection of the three most important indicators, we dynamically create three panels that are visualized in the warning message and properly adapted if necessary. For example, if a panel has to report the information on the URL, it is customized with the URL of the suspect website and the URL of the Website that is mimicked.

4 Future Work

Based on feedback received during the IFIP WG 13.2 & WG 13.5 Workshop on "Handling Security, Usability, User Experience and Reliability in User-Centered Development Processes" held in conjunction with INTERACT 2019, we are revising our proposal of intelligent warning interface.

A first suggestion we received is related to the graphical aspect of the interface, that should be able to attract user attention and communicate that it contains an alert. Actually, the interface shown at the workshop and reported in Fig. 2 is an early prototype and we are working to change its aspect.

We are also investigating how effective warning messages are constituted in terms of structure, aspect, content, and language. We started from the work in [25, 30], whose authors examined various aspects of warning design and how they affect subjective evaluations, memory, comprehension, and behavioural compliance. In fact, there is at least some involvement of perceptual and cognitive processes when making decisions with respect to warnings (e.g., the level of risk involved, whether to comply). In particular, the Communication-Human Information Processing Model (C-HIP) model [30] is widely adopted in warning design. It accounts for cognitive-affective processes, such as attitudes and motivation, which are influenced by experience as well as characteristics of the source and the channel. Based on this model, the following requirements must be considered in designing warning messages:

- *Salience*: the warning must be noticeable. It should be conspicuous enough to draw user's attention to it. In [31, 32] the authors showed that salient or conspicuous warnings increase the likelihood of reading, recall, comprehension and compliance.
- *Wordings*: the warning must be formulated according to four components: (1) signal word to attract attention, (2) identification of the hazard, (3) explanation of consequences if exposed to hazard, (4) directives to return to safety/avoiding the hazard.
- *Layout*: it is used to describe the internal characteristics of a warning label. Presenting warning text as bullets in outline form is preferred to continuous flowing text.
- *Technical Jargon*: it should be avoided as much as possible. Except if your audience is technically savvy, it is good practice to avoid technical terms. It may be hard to totally avoid some of these terms entirely, but when you *do* use them, explain what they mean in the simplest way.
- *Transparency*: when there *is a* chance of attack, communicate the potential risk, but be transparent about the uncertainty. Thus, use words like "suspect", "potential", "attackers could", etc.

We are designing a **user study** that will involve around 50 participants, representative of a large community of Internet users, both adult male and female with basic literacy level (i.e., able to use the Internet, read/write emails and perform other simple tasks with a computer). The study aims to evaluate the effectiveness of the proposed approach by comparing our intelligent warning messages to conventional phishing warning messages available in the current web browsers. As the attack has to be plausible, we plan to simulate a spear-phishing attack, which involves personalized emails or emails sent to a specifically targeted group, such as employees of a particular organization. In our case users, we will involve Internet users holding an uniba.it email account, namely people with an institutional account of the University of Bari.

5   Conclusion

In this paper, we discussed our early work on addressing phishing attack from an HCI perspective. The aim is proposing a mechanism that is able, more the currently available solutions, to attract the users' attention when they are going to fall in the attacker's trap. Our proposal has also the goal of educating the users to more safe interaction behaviors, making them able to recognize the signs of the threat and aware of the risks. Indeed, We agree with [21] that users need to understand and use systems warnings correctly in order to guarantee the efficacy of any security strategy that has been implemented. AS reported in the future work section, we are currently working at the design of an improved version of the intelligent user interface that will be tested with end users.

Acknowledgments. This work is partially supported by the Italian Ministry of University and Research (MIUR) under grant PRIN 2017 "EMPATHY: EMpowering People in deAling with internet of THings ecosYstems".

References

1. Jagatic, T.N., Johnson, N.A., Jakobsson, M., Menczer, F.: Social phishing. Commun. ACM **50**(10), 94–100 (2007)
2. APWG Anti Phishing Working Group: Phishing Attack Trends Report - 4Q 2018 (2018). http://docs.apwg.org/reports/apwg_trends_report_q4_2018.pdf
3. Thales: Insider Threat Report. https://go.thalesesecurity.com/ESG-Insider-Threat-WP.html
4. BakerHostetler: Is Your Organization Compromise Ready? 2016 Data Security Incident Response Report (2016). https://www.bakerlaw.com/files/uploads/Documents/Privacy/2016-Data-Security-Incident-Response-Report.pdf
5. Gupta, B.B., Tewari, A., Jain, A.K., Agrawal, D.P.: Fighting against phishing attacks: state of the art and future challenges. Neural Comput. Appl. **28**(12), 3629–3654 (2017). https://doi.org/10.1007/s00521-016-2275-y
6. Emigh, A.: Online identity theft: Phishing technology, chokepoints and countermeasures. ITTC Report on Online Identity Theft Technology and Counter measures (2014). http://www.anti-phishing.org/Phishingdhs-report.pdf
7. Varshney, G., Misra, M., Atrey, P.K.: A survey and classification of web phishing detection schemes. Secur. Commun. Netw. **9**(18), 6266–6284 (2016)
8. Abu-Nimeh, S., Nappa, D., Wang, X., Nair, S.: A comparison of machine learning techniques for phishing detection. In: Anti-phishing Working Groups 2nd annual eCrime Researchers Summit (eCrime 2007), pp. 60–69. ACM, New York (2007)
9. Almomani, A., Gupta, B.B., Atawneh, S., Meulenberg, A., Almomani, E.: A survey of phishing email filtering techniques. IEEE Commun. Surv. Tutor. **15**(4), 2070–2090 (2013)
10. Biran, O., Cotton, C.: Explanation and justification in machine learning: a survey. In: IJCAI-17 workshop on explainable AI (XAI 2017) (2017)
11. Wu, M.: Fighting Phishing at the User Interface. Massachusetts Institute of Technology (2006)
12. Department of Justice Federal Bureau of Investigation: FBI Says Web Spoofing Scams Are a Growing Problem (2003). http://www.fbi.gov/pressrel/pressrel03/spoofing072103.htm
13. Wu, M., Miller, R.C., Garfinkel, S.L.: Do security toolbars actually prevent phishing attacks? In: ACM SIGCHI Conference on Human Factors in Computing Systems (CHI 2006), pp. 601–610. ACM, New York (2006)
14. Herzberg, A.: Why Johnny can't surf (safely)? Attacks and defenses for web users. Comput. Secur. **28**(1–2), 63–71 (2009)
15. Dhamija, R., Tygar, J.D., Hearst, M.: Why phishing works. In: ACM SIGCHI Conference on Human Factors in Computing Systems (CHI 2006). pp. 581–590. ACM, New York, NY, USA (2006)
16. Martin, T.D.: Phishing for Answers: Exploring the Factors that Influence a Participant's Ability to Correctly Identify Email. Capella University, Minneapolis (2008)
17. McNealy, J.E.: Angling for phishers: legislative responses to deceptive e-mail. Commun. Law Policy **13**(2), 275–300 (2008)
18. Sheng, S., Holbrook, M., Kumaraguru, P., Cranor, L.F., Downs, J.: Who falls for phish? A demographic analysis of phishing susceptibility and effectiveness of interventions. In: ACM SIGCHI Conference on Human Factors in Computing Systems (CHI 2010), pp. 373–382. ACM, New York (2010)

19. Kumaraguru, P., et al.: School of phish: a real-world evaluation of anti-phishing training. In: Symposium on Usable Privacy and Security (SOUPS 2009), pp. 1–12. ACM, New York (2009)
20. Kumaraguru, P., Sheng, S., Acquisti, A., Cranor, L.F., Hong, J.: Teaching Johnny not to fall for phish. ACM Trans. Internet Technol. **10**(2), 1–31 (2010)
21. Reeder, R.W., Felt, A.P., Consolvo, S., Malkin, N., Thompson, C., Egelman, S.: An experience sampling study of user reactions to browser warnings in the field. In: ACM SIGCHI Conference on Human Factors in Computing Systems (CHI 2018), pp. 1–13. ACM, New York (2018)
22. Afroz, S., Greenstadt, R.: PhishZoo: detecting phishing websites by looking at them. In: IEEE International Conference on Semantic Computing (ICSC 2011), pp. 368–375 (2011)
23. Egelman, S., Cranor, L.F., Hong, J.: You've been warned: an empirical study of the effectiveness of web browser phishing warnings. In: ACM SIGCHI Conference on Human Factors in Computing Systems (CHI 2008), pp. 1065–1074. ACM, New York (2008)
24. IBM: IBM X-Force Threat Intelligence Index 2018. https://microstrat.com/sites/default/files/security-ibm-security-solutions-wg-research-report-77014377usen-20180329.pdf
25. Felt, A.P., et al.: Improving SSL warnings: comprehension and adherence. In: ACM Conference on Human Factors in Computing Systems (CHI 2015), pp. 2893–2902. ACM, New York (2015)
26. Adadi, A., Berrada, M.: Peeking inside the black-box: a survey on Explainable Artificial Intelligence (XAI). IEEE Access **6**, 52138–52160 (2018)
27. Jensen, M.L., Dinger, M., Wright, R.T., Thatcher, J.B.: Training to mitigate phishing attacks using mindfulness techniques. J. Manage. Inf. Syst. **34**(2), 597–626 (2017)
28. Le Page, S., Jourdan, G.-V., Bochmann, G.V., Onut, I.-V., Flood, J.: Domain classifier: compromised machines versus malicious registrations. In: Bakaev, M., Frasincar, F., Ko, I.-Y. (eds.) ICWE 2019. LNCS, vol. 11496, pp. 265–279. Springer, Cham (2019). https://doi.org/10.1007/978-3-030-19274-7_20
29. Quinlan, J.R.: Programs for Machine Learning. Morgan Kaufmann Publishers Inc., San Francisco (1993)
30. Wogalter, M.S., Conzola, V.C., Smith-Jackson, T.L.: Research-based guidelines for warning design and evaluation. Appl. Ergon. **33**(3), 219–230 (2002)
31. Strawbridge, J.A.: The influence of position, highlighting, and imbedding on warning effectiveness. Proc. Hum. Factors Soc. Annu. Meet. **30**(7), 716–720 (1986)
32. Barlow, T., Wogalter, M.S.: Alcohol beverage warnings in print advertisements. Proc. Hum. Factors Soc. Annu. Meet. **35**(6), 451–455 (1991)

On the Development of Context-Aware Augmented Reality Applications

Enes Yigitbas(✉)⓪, Ivan Jovanovikj⓪, Stefan Sauer⓪, and Gregor Engels⓪

Paderborn University, Fürstenallee 11, 33102 Paderborn, Germany
{enes.yigitbas,ivan.jovanovikj,stefan.sauer,gregor.engels}@upb.de

Abstract. Augmented Reality (AR) is a technique that enables users to interact with their physical environment through the overlay of digital information. With the spread of AR applications in various domains (e.g. product design, manufacturing or maintenance) and the introduction of concepts such as Pervasive Augmented Reality (PAR), the aspect *context-awareness* started to play an important role. By sensing the user's current context and adapting the AR application accordingly, an adequate user experience can be achieved. Due to the complex structure and composition of AR applications, their development is a challenging task. Although, context-awareness for AR systems was addressed to some extent, a systematic method for development of context-aware AR applications is not fully covered yet. Therefore, in this paper, we identify the main challenges for development of context-aware AR applications and sketch our solution idea for a model-based development framework. The benefit and applicability of our solution idea is shown on the basis of two example mobile AR applications supporting context-awareness.

Keywords: Augmented reality · Context-awareness · Model-based development

1 Introduction

Augmented Reality (AR) is a user interface metaphor, which allows for interweaving digital data with physical spaces. AR relies on the concept of overlaying digital data onto the physical world, typically in form of graphical augmentations in real-time [1]. Augmented reality has been researched for a considerable amount of time, with first implementations as early as Sutherland's head-mounted three dimensional display "The sword of Damocles" [10] from 1966. The expression *Augmented Reality* was first coined by Tom Caudell in 1992 in his work on the "Application of Heads-Up Display Technology to Manual Manufacturing Processes" [3]. In more recent years, AR technology is strongly on the rise, with many different devices available. One main technology are Head-Mounted-Displays (HMDs) like Microsoft's HoloLens[1] or the Magic Leap One[2]:

---

[1] https://www.microsoft.com/en-CY/hololens.
[2] https://www.magicleap.com/magic-leap-one.

© IFIP International Federation for Information Processing 2020
Published by Springer Nature Switzerland AG 2020
J. Abdelnour Nocera et al. (Eds.): INTERACT 2019, LNCS 11930, pp. 107–120, 2020.
https://doi.org/10.1007/978-3-030-46540-7_11

Headsets with integrated display and optics. Some of them also have built in hardware to process the programs that run on the HMD, while other headsets need to be connected to a computer and only serve as a special kind of display which also includes control functions. An alternative way in AR-technology is to use a smartphone as the main hardware. The smartphone can be worn in a headgear ("Head-mounted Smartphone"), which is not very common for AR applications yet, as many of the headgears only support VR, for example because the phone-camera's lens is simply covered by the gear. More often smartphones are used in their original purpose, as handheld AR devices.

With the spread and increasing usage of Augmented Reality (AR) techniques in different domains, the need for context-awareness in AR was underlined in previous work [4]. Supporting context-awareness, can greatly enhance user experience in AR applications, for example by adjusting to the individual needs of each user. It also makes the usage more intuitive and effective: The more the application can adjust to the user and his situation, the more natural the AR is experienced and the more ergonomic it is to work with.

However, due to the complex structure (tasks, scenes) and composition (inter-relations between real and virtual information objects) of AR applications [11], the development of context-aware AR applications is a challenging task. While context-aware AR applications were introduced for specific application domains, e.g. maintenance [16], a systematic method for supporting the efficient development of context-aware AR applications is not fully covered yet. Therefore, in this paper, we discuss the main challenges in developing context-aware AR applications and sketch a first solution idea for a model-based development framework for context-aware augmented reality applications.

The rest of the paper is structured as follows: In Sect. 2, we discuss main challenges in developing context-aware AR applications. In Sect. 3, we present architectural patterns as basic solution concepts for addressing these challenges. Section 4 provides an overview of our integrated model-based framework supporting the development of context-aware AR applications. In Sect. 5, we present case studies to show the applicability of our framework. Section 6 gives an overview of related work. Finally, Sect. 7 concludes our work with an outlook on future work.

2   Challenges

The challenges in developing context-aware AR applications can be divided up in to three main categories: multi-platform capability, adaptation capability, and round-tripping capability. In the following, we describe each category in more detail.

2.1   Multi-platform

An augmented reality application can be used across heterogeneous computing platforms spanning over head-mounted display (HMD) devices to mobile hand held devices. There are a number of AR capable devices on the market which are developed by different companies and organizations. Target devices could be smartphones, tablets or HMDs as the Microsoft Hololens, RealWear Glasses or Google Glass Enterprise Edition, just to mention a few. The cost of a device, its comfort in using it and the ability of a device to help the user accomplish her task are some of the reasons that influences the type of equipment that different users and organizations use to acquire them. In a real world scenario, most users and organizations would like to have the freedom of choosing devices for task execution on an AR application which are most suitable for them if they require to use AR solutions. Mostly, their concerns are to have a mixture of several devices to suit the varying nature of tasks available and also to meet their budget constraints. Each computing platform can have different properties regarding hardware and sensor, operating system, used AR SDKs etc. To support multi-platform AR experience across heterogeneous computing platforms, an efficient way of developing various AR applications is needed.

2.2 Adaptation

For supporting context-aware and adaptive AR applications various aspects have to be taken into account.

First of all, context monitoring is an important prerequisite for enabling context-aware applications in general. An important challenge in this regard is to continuously observe the context-of-use of an AR application through various sensors. The context-of-use can be described through different characteristics regarding user (physical, emotional, preferences etc.), platform (Hololens, Hand-held, etc.), and environment (real vs. virtual environmental information). Due to the rich context dimension which is spanning over the real world and virtual objects, it is a complex task to track and relate the relevant context information to each other. The mixture of real (position, posture, emotion, etc.) and virtual (coordinates, view angle, walk-through, etc.) context information additionally increases the aspect of context management compared to classical context-aware applications like in the web or mobile context.

Based on the collected context information, a decision making process is required to analyze and decide whether conditions and constraints are fulfilled to trigger specific adaptation operations on the AR application. In general, an important challenge is to cope with conflicting adaptation rules which aim at different adaptation goals. This problem is even more emphasized in the case of AR applications as we need to ensure a consistent display between the real world entities and virtual overlay information. For the decision making step it is also important to decide about a reasoning technique like rule-based or learning-based to provide a performant and scalable solution.

As AR applications consist of a complex structure and composition, an extremely high number of various adaptations is possible. The adaptations should cover text, symbols, 2D images and videos, as well as 3D models and animations. In this regard, many adaptation combinations and modality changes increase the complexity of the adaptation process.

2.3 Round-Trip

Beside the before mentioned challenges, it is important for a context-aware AR application to support the flexible usage of various information objects. On the one hand, information objects can be text, symbols, 2D and 3D objects which are predefined and available in an existing object repository. On the other hand, it should be also possible to digitize existing real world physical objects, e.g. through a 3D scan, so that further objects can be stored in the object repository and reused at run-time. We call this flexible way of transferring real world physical objects in to a repository and making them reusable again as round-trip. In order to support such a round-trip for the development of context-aware AR applications, a solution should enable the following steps: scan physical objects, refine object model, store object model in repository. Beside that, the import and usage of the created object models the development environment should be supported.

3 Solution Idea

In order to support the development of context-aware augmented reality applications, we have identified basic architectural patterns to address the identified challenges: Multi-platform, Adaptation and Round-trip capabilities.

3.1 Multi-platform Capability

For increasing the efficiency of multi-platform user interface development in the context of AR, we envision to establish a model-based development process. Based on the *CAMELEON Reference Framework* [2], as described in Fig. 1, we propose a step wise model-based development process.

The top layer Task & Concept includes a task model that is used for the hierarchical description of the activities and actions of individual users of the AR user interface. The abstract user interface (AUI) is described in the form of a dialogue model that specifies the user's interaction with the user interface independent of specific technology. The platform specific representation of the user interface is described by the concrete user interface (CUI), which is specified by a presentation model. The lowest layer of the framework is the final user interface (FUI) for the target platform. The vertical dimension describes the path from abstract to concrete models. Here, a top-down approach is followed, in which the abstract description of relevant information about the user interface (AUI) is enriched to more sophisticated models (CUI) through model-to-model transformations (M2M). Subsequently, the refined models are transformed (model-to-code transformation, M2C) to produce the final augmented reality user interface (AR FUI). Based on this architectural pattern, it is possible to enable multi-platform capability for the different UIs that are generated during the development process.

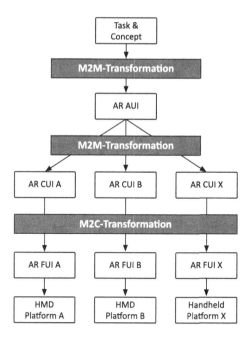

Fig. 1. Multi-platform support

3.2 Adaptation Capability

Based on our previous work in the area of UI adaptation for web and mobile apps [12], we propose an extended version of IBM's MAPE-K architecture (shown in Fig. 2) to support context-aware AR applications.

AS depicted in Fig. 2, the MAPE-K architecture consists of two main parts *Adaptation Manager* and *Managed Element*. In our case, the *Managed Element* is an AR application consisting of *Tasks*, *Scenes* and *Interrelations* between them. The *Adaptation Manager* is responsible for monitoring and adapting the AR application through sensors and effectors in order to provide a highly usable AR experience. In the following, the functionality of each sub-component of the *Adaptation Manager* is briefly described.

The monitor component is responsible for observing the context information. Context information changes are then evaluated by the analyze component to decide whether adaptation is needed. If so, the planning of an adaptation schedule is done by the plan component. Finally, the adaptation operations are performed by the execute component, so that an adapted UI can be presented. The knowledge management base is responsible for storing data that is logged over time and can be used for inferring future adaptation operations.

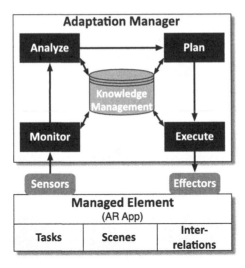

Fig. 2. Adaptation support

3.3 Round-Trip Capability

For supporting round-trip functionality in a context-aware AR application, we envision to establish a client-server architecture that enables digitization, storage and reuse of physical objects in an object repository. For this purpose, as depicted in Fig. 3, we propose a *AR/VR Server* consisting of an *AR/VR Object Repository*. This repository can contain already predefined virtual objects. On the other hand it is possible to use the *AR Client*, e.g. a handheld AR device, to scan and digitize physical real world objects. These objects can be refined and add to the local AR/VR repository which is synchronized with the central *AR/VR Object Repository*. This enables the user to transfer physical objects into the repository, in order to build an object basis as well as projects the repository objects back into reality via augmentation.

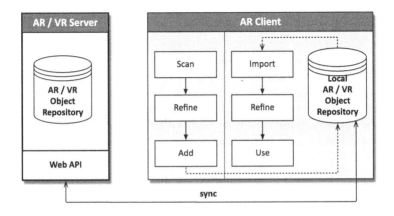

Fig. 3. Round-trip support

4   Model-Based Framework for Context-Aware AR Application

In the previous section, we have presented different architectural patterns for supporting the development of context-aware AR applications. While these patterns address basic solution concepts for tackling the different challenges, it is important to design an integrated framework which combines the several aspects of multi-platform capability, adaptation capability and round-trip capability. For this reason, we propose an integrated model-based framework for context-aware AR applications. Our framework is depicted in Fig. 4 and consists of the previously described solution patterns.

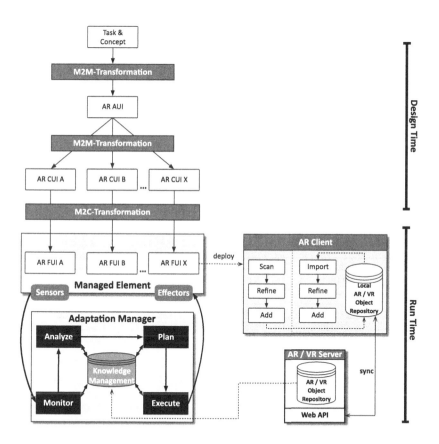

Fig. 4. Model-based development framework for context-aware AR apps

At design time, the described model-based development process supports to generate the final AR user interfaces for various target platforms. The generated final UI is deployed to a specific AR client which enables the described round-trip functionality at run-time. Also, the generated final UI of the AR application is monitored and adapted through the *Adaptation Manager* at run-time as described in the previous section. In addition to the provided framework, we elaborate on the adaptation process as it is a crucial prerequisite for enabling context-aware AR applications.

To address the adaptation process at different development stages, we combine our previous work on model-driven development of adaptive UIs for web and mobile apps [12] with an existing method for structured design of AR UIs [11]. As shown in Fig. 5, our solution concept addresses three different aspects: *AR UI*, *Context*, and *Adaptation*. Regarding the *AR UI* aspect, shown in the leftmost column in Fig. 5, we rely on the approach and the *SSIML/AR* language of Vitzhum [11]. *SSIML/AR (Scene Structure and Integration Modeling/Augmented Reality)* is a visual modeling language which provides model elements for modeling virtual objects and groups in a virtual scene. Additionally, the relations between application classes and the 3D scene can also be specified. Using *SSIML/AR*, an abstract specification of the user interface of the AR application is created. This *Abstract AR UI Model* is the input for the *AR UI Generator*, which generates the *Final AR UI*. In order to support the creation of context-aware AR apps, we complement the development method with two additional aspects, namely the *Context* and *Adaptation*, originally presented in [12].

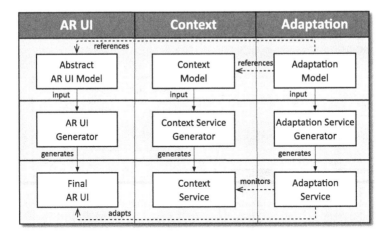

Fig. 5. Model-based solution architecture for adaptive AR apps

The *Context* aspect serves to characterize the dynamically changing context-of-use parameters by providing an abstract specification in terms of a *Context Model*. Based on the *Context Model*, the *Context Service Generator* generates the *Context Service* which monitors context information like brightness, acceleration or noise level. The *Adaptation* aspect addresses the specification of the adaptation logic in terms of abstract AR UI adaptation rules represented as the

Adaptation Model. The specified AR UI adaptation rules reference the *Context Model* to define the context constraints for triggering adaptation rules and they also reference the *Abstract AR UI Model* to define which AR UI elements are scope of a UI adaptation change. The *Adaptation Model* is the input for the *Adaptation Service Generator* which generates an *Adaptation Service.* At run-time, the *Adaptation Service* monitors the context information provided by the *Context Service* and adapts the *Final AR UI.*

5   Case Studies

In this section, two case studies are presented which show the benefit of using our model-based development framework for developing context-aware AR applications. The first case study deals with the development of a context-aware mobile AR app which supports UI adaptation capabilities. The second case study shows an example implementation of our object repository supporting the mentioned round-trip capability for scanning and reusing various objects in AR applications.

5.1   Context-Aware Mobile AR App Supporting Adaptation Capability

For addressing the adaptation capability, described in Sect. 2, we shortly present the implementation of a context-aware mobile AR application for printer maintenance tasks. Usually, printers have to be maintained and various tasks like refilling paper or changing cartridges should be performed on a regular basis. For such tasks, the printer device usually comes up with a manual. However, most users find it cumbersome to read through the whole manual to accomplish straightforward tasks. Due to this reason and to illustrate the benefit of context-aware AR applications, we implemented an AR application for this example scenario by using our development framework. The context-aware printer maintenance AR (CAPMAR) app makes use of the used smartphone's hardware sensors to observe various context characteristics about the user, platform, and environment. Beside that, we have a preliminary starting questionnaire where newly starting users of the CAPMAR app are asked about their task experience, age etc. Based on those static and dynamically observed context information at run-time, the CAPMAR app is able to trigger AR interfaces adaptations to better suit the context-of-use. Figure 6 is showing a screenshot from the CAPMAR app, where on the left app screen a shorter help message is shown, while on the right screen for a beginner user who is not familiar with the task, a more detailed description of the task is depicted. In summary, the implementation of the CAPMAR app, shows the interface adaptation capability of our model-based development framework for context-aware AR applications.

5.2   Object Repository Supporting Round-Trip Capability

In order to address the round-trip capability, described in Sect. 3.3, we have implemented an object repository which supports the digitization of physical

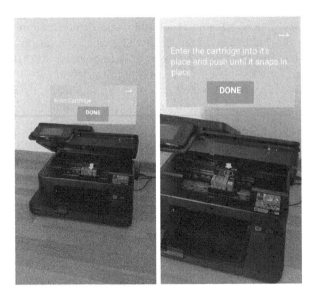

Fig. 6. Case study 1: context-aware AR printer maintenance app

objects through photogrammetry. As illustrated on the left of Fig. 7, we can use third party photogrammetry applications to scan a real object and make a 3D model out of it. The derived 3D object model can be imported into our object repository which enables to mange various of those 3D objects. The object repository is implemented as a web server and supports the persistence of various objects in varying levels of quality detail. Upon the need of the objects, they can be searched and reused based on our mobile client which can position the derived objects in the real scene. In summary, the combination of such an object repository with the concept of context-awareness brings many advantages to ease the developers work in devising context-aware AR apps.

6   Related Work

In previous work, different approaches were introduced to address the development of context-aware augmented reality applications. In the following, according the challenges introduced in Sect. 2, we analyze the related work regarding context-awareness in augmented reality applications, multi-platform capability, and object round-tripping.

While context-awareness has been exploited in various types of applications including web [12], mobile [14], cross-channel [15] and virtual reality [13] to improve the usability of an interactive system by adapting its user interface, there are only few existing works focusing on the topic of context-awareness in augmented reality.

In [4], the concept of Pervasive Augmented Reality (PAR) is introduced. A taxonomy for PAR and context-aware AR that classifies context sources and

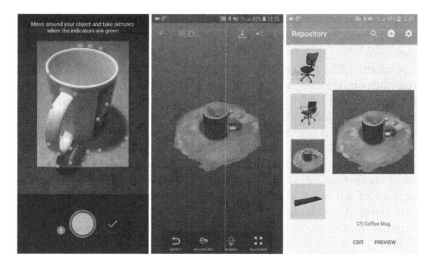

Fig. 7. Case study 2: object repository for AR apps

targets is presented. The context sources are classified as human, environmental and system factors. As apparent in the title, Grubert's work treats Augmented Reality, here with special regards to pervasive Augmented Reality.

Context-aware Mobile Augmented Reality (CAMAR) [9] is an approach on context-awareness in mobile AR focusing on user context, which is measured using the user's mobile device. It enables the user to customize the presentation of virtual content and to share this information with other users selectively, depending on the context. Furthermore, a framework called UCAM (Unified Context-aware Application Model) [5] can be used to create CAMAR-enabled applications. UCAM is a framework which beside the acquisition, process, and awareness of contextual information provides also a unified way of representation with respect to user, content, and environment.

The framework presented in [6] focuses on context-aware adaptation of interfaces in mixed reality, with the main adaptation points being what content is displayed, where it is shown and how much information of it is displayed. It is designed to adjust the content display depending on the user's tasks and their cognitive load and archives this using a combination of rule-based decisions and combinatorial optimization. The framework uses parameters about the applications that are to be displayed as input additionally to the context-specific parameters to achieve a fitting layout optimisation. The framework is mentioning mixed reality as its base, but regarding that it shows contents in the real world and does not create a whole new virtual world, it can safely be said that AR is supported.

While above mentioned approaches address the development of context-aware applications, the main focus is not lying on a model-based development framework for context-aware AR applications. As such, the required concerns and features regarding context-awareness and interfaces adaptation are mostly manually implemented while our solution idea is aiming a model-based approach that increases reusability, maintainability, and portability of the AR app for different target platforms. The AR Foundation project[3], aims to the creation of AR apps that run both on iOS and Android. It provides a common API which covers the core functionality of both Android ARCore[4] and iOS ARKit[5], thus making it possible to develop AR applications for both platforms from a single code base.

Beside the above described approaches focusing on context-awareness in augmented reality applications, we shortly describe prior work that addresses the topics of round-trip capability and object repositories for prototyping and development of context-aware AR applications. One important resource to assist the development of AR applications is given by object repositories such as Google Poly[6] or Unity Asset Store[7]. Main idea of such object repositories is to provide a public repository for all sorts of assets (images, 3D models, sound and visual effects, etc.) which can be reused in the development of augmented reality applications for different domains and in various projects. Beside that, existing approaches like DART [7] or ProtoAR [8] aim to support the rapid prototyping of AR applications. While these approaches ease the prototyping and development of AR applications even for non-technical developers, their focus is not lying on support for addressing context-awareness and interface adaptation. Therefore, our model-based development framework for context-aware AR applications makes use of synergy effects between existing prototyping approaches and object repositories that are combined with a model-based development approach for context-aware AR apps.

7   Conclusion and Outlook

This paper discusses the main challenges in developing context-aware augmented reality applications and presents architectural solution patterns to address them. Based on the identified architectural solution patterns, we propose an integrated model-based development framework for context-aware AR applications. Furthermore, we elaborate on the adaptation process and propose a model-based solution architecture for the development of adaptive AR applications. At the end, we show that our framework can be used for the development of context-aware AR applications.

In future work, we plan to implement tool-support for model-based development of context-aware AR applications. Our goal is to support the efficient development of context-aware AR applications for different application scenarios covering different target platforms.

---

[3] https://unity.com/unity/features/arfoundation.

[4] https://developers.google.com/ar.

[5] https://developer.apple.com/augmented-reality/.

[6] https://poly.google.com/.

[7] https://assetstore.unity.com/.

References

1. Azuma, R.T.: A survey of augmented reality. Presence: Teleoper. Virtual Environ. **6**(4), 355–385 (1997)
2. Calvary, G., Coutaz, J., Thevenin, D., Limbourg, Q., Bouillon, L., Vanderdonckt, J.: A unifying reference framework for multi-target user interfaces. Interact. Comput. **15**(3), 289–308 (2003)
3. Caudell, T.P., Mizell, D.W.: Augmented reality: an application of heads-up display technology to manual manufacturing processes. In: Proceedings of the Twenty-Fifth Hawaii International Conference on System Sciences, vol. 2, pp. 659–669, January 1992
4. Grubert, J., et al.: Towards pervasive augmented reality: context-awareness in augmented reality. IEEE Trans. Vis. Comput. Graph. **23**(6), 1706–1724 (2017)
5. Hong, D., Shin, C., Oh, S., Woo, W.: A new paradigm for user interaction in ubiquitous computing environment. In: ISUVR 2006, pp. 41–44 (2006)
6. Lindlbauer, D., Feit, A.M., Hilliges, O.: Context-aware online adaptation of mixed reality interfaces. In: Proceedings of the 32nd Annual ACM Symposium on User Interface Software and Technology, UIST 2019, New Orleans, LA, USA, 20–23 October 2019, pp. 147–160 (2019)
7. MacIntyre, B., Gandy, M., Bolter, J.D., Dow, S., Hannigan, B.: DART: the designer's augmented reality toolkit. In: 2003 IEEE/ACM International Symposium on Mixed and Augmented Reality (ISMAR 2003), 7–10 October 2003, Tokyo, Japan, pp. 329–330 (2003)
8. Nebeling, M., Nebeling, J., Yu, A., Rumble, R.: Protoar: rapid physical-digital prototyping of mobile augmented reality applications. In: Proceedings of the 2018 CHI Conference on Human Factors in Computing Systems, CHI 2018, Montreal, QC, Canada, 21–26 April 2018, p. 353 (2018)
9. Oh, S., Woo, W., et al.: Camar: context-aware mobile augmented reality in smart space. Proc. IWUVR **9**, 48–51 (2009)
10. Sutherland, I.E.: A head-mounted three dimensional display. In: Proceedings of the Fall Joint Computer Conference, Part I. pp. 757–764, 9–11 December 1968. AFIPS 1968 (Fall, part I). ACM, New York, NY, USA (1968)
11. Vitzthum, A.: SSIML/AR: a visual language for the abstract specification of augmented reality user interfaces. In: IEEE Symposium on 3D User Interfaces, pp. 135–142 (2006)
12. Yigitbas, E., Stahl, H., Sauer, S., Engels, G.: Self-adaptive UIs: integrated model-driven development of UIs and their adaptations. In: Anjorin, A., Espinoza, H. (eds.) ECMFA 2017. LNCS, vol. 10376, pp. 126–141. Springer, Cham (2017). https://doi.org/10.1007/978-3-319-61482-3_8
13. Yigitbas, E., Heindörfer, J., Engels, G.: A context-aware virtual reality first aid training application. In: Proceedings of Mensch und Computer 2019, Hamburg, Germany, 8–11 September 2019, pp. 885–888 (2019)
14. Yigitbas, E., Josifovska, K., Jovanovikj, I., Kalinci, F., Anjorin, A., Engels, G.: Component-based development of adaptive user interfaces. In: Proceedings of the ACM SIGCHI Symposium on Engineering Interactive Computing Systems, EICS 2019, Valencia, Spain, 18–21 June 2019, pp. 13:1–13:7 (2019)

15. Yigitbas, E., Sauer, S.: Engineering context-adaptive UIs for task-continuous cross-channel applications. In: Bogdan, C., et al. (eds.) HCSE/HESSD -2016. LNCS, vol. 9856, pp. 281–300. Springer, Cham (2016). https://doi.org/10.1007/978-3-319-44902-9_18
16. Zhu, J., et al.: A context-aware augmented reality assisted maintenance system. Int. J. Compu. Integr. Manuf. **28**(2), 213–225 (2015)

Towards Identification of Patterns Aligning Security and Usability

Bilal Naqvi$^{(\boxtimes)}$ ⓘ, Jari Porras ⓘ, Shola Oyedeji ⓘ, and Mehar Ullah ⓘ

Software Engineering, LENS, LUT University, 53850 Lappeenranta, Finland
syed.naqvi@student.lut.fi

Abstract. Academic research and existing implementations of various systems and services identify instances of conflict between security and usability. Engineering the right trade-offs between security and usability is often not an easy task. Engineering of such trade-offs is mainly reliant on developers' skills, who are either experts in security or usability. This research aims to assist the developers in engineering the right trade-offs by proposing the use of patterns. Patterns provide benefits like means of common vocabulary, shared documentation, reuse, among others. The use of patterns can assist security and usability developers by influencing their decision-making abilities when dealing with conflicts in other but similar context of use. For the identification of such patterns, the paper presents a three-stage methodology. To instantiate the methodology, a case study was conducted whose results are also presented in the paper.

Keywords: Security · Usability · Usable security · Patterns

1 Introduction

Security and usability are considered as conflicting goals [1]. The trade-offs between the two are discussed at different forums not limited to cyber-security and Human Computer Interaction (HCI). Typical examples of the security and usability conflict include (1) complex password guidelines having an impact on memorability, (2) implementation of password masking to protect against 'shoulder surfing attacks' but at the cost of feedback (usability element), among others.

Traditionally security and usability have evolved independently and as different domains, therefore, expertise in both security and usability is hard to find in one person [2]. Despite this, the developers are ones who face most of the criticism when the security solutions are unusable, or when usability features pose a threat to systems' security. The domain considering the integration of principles of security and aspects of usability is known as *usable security*.

The early efforts in the field of usable security date back to 1998 when different properties of usability problems relevant to the development of security systems were identified [3]. Despite this recognition, state of the art concerning usable security still has some catching up to do. Practices and trends followed in the large organizations reveal a

J. Abdelnour Nocera et al. (Eds.): INTERACT 2019, LNCS 11930, pp. 121–132, 2020.
https://doi.org/10.1007/978-3-030-46540-7_12

lack of motivation in considering usable security as a quality dimension [4]. One possible reason for this state is the cost associated with usable security [19]. The implementation of security due to the constantly evolving threat environment and usability due to rapid technological advancements has been so demanding that it leaves less time and costs to manage the trade-offs between the two. Among the other reasons for the current state of the art, it is imperative to discuss the following.

- *Different perceptions concerning security and usability*: The community has a different opinion concerning the existence of trade-offs between security and usability. Most of the research argues the existence of trade-offs between security and usability [5, 6]. However, in parallel with the research establishing the existence of the trade-offs, there is some research classifying security and usability trade-offs as mere myths [7, 8]. When the opinion on the existence of the problem is divided, then it is difficult to effectively contribute towards solving it.
- *Varying types of users:* In the community of users of the same device or application, opinions and requirements concerning security and privacy differ. Therefore, it is difficult to cater to the requirements of such a diverse category of users, which further complicates the task of finding common ground between security and usability and delivering a usable secure system.
- *Studying the conflicts by different communities in silos*: Various communities and interest groups have been studying usable security in silos, independently from each other. Some of these include, *(1)* SOUPS (Symposium on Usable Security and Privacy), small community studying trends, avenues and advancements in usable security. Much of the content is tactical, rather than being strategic, *(2)* The cybersecurity community dealing with the wider scope of security services; usability is a minor concern for this community, *(3)* The software engineering community where security and usability are considered as quality characteristics. Some of the standards provide contradictory perceptions and models for the same software quality characteristics, e.g. definition of usability in ISO 9126 and ISO 9241-11, *(4)* The HCI community, where the researchers try to explain from a cognitive perspective how users make poor security decisions leading to system compromises. There is no medium for collaboration that enables views from different communities and perspectives to be incorporated.
- *Ineffective joint working groups*: Because of independent activities, there is a lack of joint efforts concerning usable security. However, there exist multiple working groups specifically on usable security, but combining their findings to come up with a strategic vision for usable security, remains a challenge.
- *Lack of strategic approach*: Much of the work related to usable security suffers from a cosmetic approach that is the solutions are limited to specific problems, rather than contributing towards the management of the conflicts in general [2]. For example, there was a perception that CAPTCHA (*Completely Automated Public Turing Test to Tell Computers and Humans Apart*) poses *readability* problems for the users, therefore, new CAPTCHAS were developed that allow the user to select relevant images in response to the challenge. The question that remains valid for the community to address is, '*do we need CAPTCHAS?*'. The prime purpose of CAPTCHA is to protect against denial of service (DoS) attacks, which is the responsibility of the service provider, and then why the user should bear the burden to deal with the CAPTCHA

especially when they cause deviation from the users' primary task. Likewise, the majority of the work on usable security has been on the operational and tactical level and therefore, has a cosmetic effect on the usable security problem. However, what is required in this regard are the long term and strategic solutions, for example, a requirement-engineering framework for aligning security and usability during the phases of the system development lifecycle (SDLC).

Moreover, one aspect on which there is a consensus among different groups working on usable security is to focus on learning and assisting the developers in handling the security and usability conflicts. This forms the primary research question addressed in this paper, which is *'how to assist security and usability developers in handling the conflicts and identifying suitable trade-offs while enabling learning in a specific context of use?'*. This research advocates the concept of *'usable security by design'*, which is aimed at assisting the developers in handling the conflicts and identifying suitable trade-offs by using design patterns. Each design pattern solves a recurring design problem in a particular context of use. Using the patterns' approach can be advantageous not only for the developers but for the organizations as well. Software development organizations can also contribute to the catalog of patterns, based on previous experiences from the projects. Furthermore, using the patterns while ensuring effective management of the trade-offs does not affect the timely completion and costs associated with the project.

There are some existing usable security design patterns, but there is a need to collect those patterns, add them to a catalog and disseminate the catalog among the developers and designers. Furthermore, it is imperative to identify more patterns to be added to the catalog. For identifying more usable security patterns, the proposal for a three-stage methodology is presented in this paper. The remainder of the paper is organized as follows. Section 2 presents the background and literature review. Section 3 presents the proposed methodology for the identification of usable security patterns from existing implementations. Section 4 presents a case study to instantiate the proposed methodology. Section 5 presents the discussion and avenues for future investigation identified after the workshop, and Sect. 6 concludes the paper.

2 Background and Literature Review

In line with the research question addressed in this paper, the literature review was conducted considering the following objectives.

1. To rationalize the use of patterns as a way of assisting developers in handling interdisciplinary conflicts e.g. security and usability conflicts.
2. To identify existing usable security patterns (if any) and methodologies for identification for such patterns.

The authors [9] state, "insufficient communication with users produces a lack of user-centered design in security mechanisms". Both usability and security professionals recognize the importance of incorporating their concerns throughout the design cycle and acknowledge the need for an iterative rather than a linear design process. The use of patterns allows the concerns from both security and usability viewpoints to be incorporated right from the start of system development lifecycle. Patterns' ability to be improved over time and incorporate multiple viewpoints make them suitable for interdisciplinary fields like usable security [1]. Handling the security and usability concerns earlier in the development lifecycle helps in saving significant costs and delays associated with re-work.

An architect Christopher Alexander in the book 'A Pattern Language' originally introduced the concept of patterns [10]. Deriving inspiration from this, the same concept was implemented in computer science particularly in software engineering to assist the designers of the system, while providing guidelines and high-level principles. A similar concept was introduced in HCI to assist the development of user interface design (e.g. [11, 12]).

Each pattern expresses a relation between three things, *context, problem,* and *solution.* Patterns provide real solutions, not abstract principles, by explicitly mentioning the context and problem and summarizing the rationale for their effectiveness. Since the patterns provide a generic "core" solution, its use can vary from one implementation to another.

Furthermore, the patterns have three dimensions: descriptive, normative, and communicative [17]. From the perspective of usable security, the communicative dimensions of the patterns enable different communities to discuss design issues and solutions. Patterns also prove effective in the domains, which lack an existing body of knowledge; in such cases, the patterns assist in identifying effective practices as they emerge and capture them as objects for discussion, scrutiny, and modification [17].

In line with the second objective of the literature review, it was identified that the authors [13] while listing 20 usable security patterns also presented the results after analysis of commonly used software browsers like Internet Explorer, Mozilla Firefox and email clients like Microsoft Outlook. It was revealed that the identified patterns had a 61.67% application in the analyzed software implementations. The authors state "patterns make sense and can be useful guide for software developers". However, the work was limited to listing the patterns and justifying their usage.

The authors [14] presented a list of patterns to align security and usability. They classified the patterns into two categories: data sanitization patterns and secure messaging patterns. Different patterns listed include, 'explicit user audit', 'complete delete', 'create keys when needed', among others.

The authors [15] proposed a set of user interface design patterns for designing information security feedback based on elements of user interface design. Furthermore, the authors created prototypes incorporating the user interface patterns in the security feedback to conduct a laboratory study. The results of the study showed that incorporating the elements of usability interface design patterns could help in making security feedbacks more meaningful and effective.

The authors [1] presented a methodology for deriving usable security patterns during the requirements engineering stage of system development. The methodology relies on handling the conflicts during the early stages of system development and documenting the suitable trade-offs in the form of design patterns for reuse. What distinguishes the methodology presented in this paper from the work [1] is that the methodology discussed in this paper focuses on identifying and documenting instances of good implementations by experienced developers in the form of design patterns. This is more of a bottom-up approach involving the identification of the patterns from existing implementations. However, the work [1] focuses on the creation of new patterns based on system requirements where possible trade-offs are identified and managed. The managed trade-offs are documented as patterns for implementation in the specific project and reuse by other developers.

3 Methodology for the Identification of Usable Security Patterns

In this section, the proposed three-stage methodology for the identification of usable security patterns is presented. As stated earlier, the methodology is based on identifying new patterns from existing implementations, which are setting good practices in the industry (*see* Fig. 1). This methodology provides uniform means to identify new patterns, and an opportunity for various stakeholders to contribute towards identification of the patterns and building the usable security patterns catalog. Particularly, from the industrial perspective, it can enable documenting new patterns from the implementations by experienced developers, thereby facilitating the learning and training of new developers.

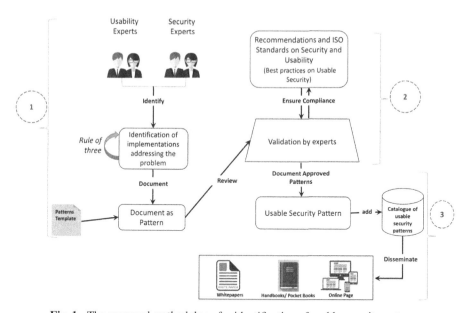

Fig. 1. The proposed methodology for identification of usable security patterns

- **Stage-1**: The first stage involves the selection of a common usable security problem. For the selection of a usable security problem, the experts can utilize one of the instruments such as surveys involving end-users, cognitive walkthroughs, heuristic evaluations, to mention a few. The next step is to identify existing implementations addressing the problem. Since the implementations can have different ways of approaching the problem, therefore, to document the best implementation as a pattern it is imperative to fulfill the '*Rule of Three*'. The rule of three requires at least three instances of similar implementations before a pattern could be identified and documented [17]. Once three instances of similar implementations for a particular problem are identified, the pattern is documented on a standard template. The details of usable security patterns' template are presented elsewhere [16]. Furthermore, selection of the best implementation is mainly based on the expertise of the professionals who are identifying it, however, to formalize the process it can also include evaluating the implementation with respect to a pre-defined set of heuristics. Defining such a set of heuristics for the evaluation would be considered as a part of the future work.

- **Stage 2**: The second stage involves a review of the newly documented pattern by one or more experts in the field. This stage involves activities like selection of expert(s) and gathering the reviews. Based on reviews the pattern is either accepted, which means it is ready to be finalized (*Stage 3*), or require modification, which means it goes back for modification to the experts who identified it during Stage 1, and in other cases, it may be rejected, which means it is discarded. The review by experts besides validation of the pattern has two advantages, (1) ensuring compliance with the underlying standards and best practices concerning security and usability, and (2) ensuring that the solution proposed in the pattern manages the trade-off effectively. The expert(s) review concerning each pattern is recorded on a checklist (see Table 1).

Table 1. Usable security pattern review checklist

Usable security pattern review checklist									
Description: For the pattern under consideration fill in the columns below. Accessing ISO standards on security and usability is highly recommended to ensure compliance									
Name of the pattern	Relevant to usable security		Effectively manages the trade-off			Compliance with the standards an best practices			Decision	Additional recommendations
l*Unique name of the pattern */	Y	N	Y	N	Y/N	Y	N	Y/N	☐ Accept ☐ Modify ☐ Reject	Include recommendations for improvement of pattern, proposal for modification, compliance to the standard, reasons for rejection, etc.

- **Stage 3**: This stage comprises the following activities subject to the decision by the expert(s):

  - *Accept:* The accepted patterns are added to the catalog. The patterns in the catalog can be disseminated among the community of developers and designers. The ways of disseminating the patterns include online pages, pocketbook for developers, and whitepapers.

- *Modify:* The documented pattern is referred back to the security and usability experts who identified it. The proposal for modification is considered and after necessary amendments, the pattern is subjected to review for the second time.
- *Reject:* The rejected patterns are discarded; however, the recommendations are considered for compliance in the other identified patterns with similar as well as the other context of use.

4   Instantiating the Methodology: A Case Study

To instantiate the methodology and identify a usable security pattern from existing implementations, a case study was conducted. The participants in the case study were the members of the software engineering laboratory at LUT University. Participation in the case study was voluntary. The objective behind the case study was to identify instances of good implementations by experienced developers, which set best practices in the field concerning the problem described below.

Case Description:
Mobile devices, particularly smartphones and tablets have become an inseparable companion for human users, as they have a wide range of features not just limited to communication. With such increased usage, we have seen an increase in cases of loss/theft of mobile devices, which ultimately leads to data breaches.

Consider a scenario when someone's smartphone is lost. Even if the lost smartphone it was locked, the victim would still be worried about ways in which an adversary could bypass the authentication mechanism and get access to the device. Access to the device could mean a breach of privacy and identity (if payment options were linked to the lost device). The authors [18] report a user study revealing that 50% of the respondents did not feel protected in case of loss/theft of their smartphone. Based on the scenario, the following problem statement was formulated.

Problem Statement:
In case of loss/theft of the users' device, the data on the device increases the impact of loss in the form of breach of privacy. The user needs to have trust and protection feelings to be able to use the device for personal/work purposes.

Stages of Case Study:
- **Stage 1**: This first stage involved the selection of the usable security problem. The results of a survey [18] led to the selection of the problem. While identifying the implementations addressing this problem, a solution 'remote data deletion' was identified. The next step involved the application of the 'rule of three'. Once three similar implementations addressing the problem were identified, the pattern (presented in Fig. 2) was documented on the standardized template. The solution offered by the pattern for the problem stated above is to "Offer the user with remote deletion functionality hosted by the mobile vendor or mobile service provider via a usable secure interface".

A secure service available online will work in this regard. It should offer the remote deletion by invoking the restore factory settings procedure, which would erase all the information from the device in case of loss/theft. This procedure not only ensures the security of data but also incorporates the human aspect of security, achieving human satisfaction and trust (elements of the global usability).

- **Title:** Data Deletion Pattern
- **Classification:** Data Protection, Device protection
- **Prologue:** To reduce the impact of loss in case of loss/theft of a device carrying sensitive personal/business information.
- **Problem statement**: In case of loss/theft of the users' device, the data on the device increases the impact of loss in the form of breach of privacy. The user needs to have trust and protection feelings to be able to use the device for personal/work purposes.
- **Context of Use:** Whenever there is loss/theft of device carrying user's data, which can lead to a breach of data.
- **Affected Sub Characteristics:** The sub- characteristics of usability and security being affected/involved when this pattern is applied.
  - Usability: satisfaction, trust, *efficiency in use*
  - Security: privacy, confidentiality, integrity
- **Solution:** Offer the User with remote deletion functionality hosted by the mobile vendor or mobile service provider via a usable secure interface.
- **Discussion:** Even if the lost smartphone was locked, the human user can still be bothered by breach of their privacy and the device's security. However, when the data has been removed from the device, the impact of loss can be minimized to an exclusively monetary loss.
- **Type of service**: Mobile devices or similar used in the same context.
- *Target Users: developers, designers*
- **Epilogue:** Improved data protection and reduced impact of loss.
- **Related Patterns:** Can be added later from the catalog.

Fig. 2. Data deletion pattern

Implementations of this pattern are available in the form of a "remote data deletion" functionality made available by smartphone manufacturers like Samsung and Apple for their users. Now the question arises who will use this pattern when this feature is already implemented? One scenario for the application of this pattern is in the case of other mobile devices including PDAs for inventory records, GPS, etc.

It is imperative to state that as per classification, the pattern (presented in Fig. 2) is a data/device protection usable security pattern. Other classifications of usable security patterns include usable authentication, usable security interface, among others. For example, a usable security interface pattern is presented in [16].

- **Stage 2**: This stage involved the validation of the pattern by the experts. It is pertinent to state that the pattern presented in Fig. 2 is a validated version of the pattern after reviewing by the experts. The items in *italic* were added based on experts' recommendations. The pattern review checklist from one of the experts is presented in Fig. 3.

Usable Security Pattern Review Checklist									
Description: For the pattern under consideration fill in the columns below. Accessing ISO standards on security and usability is highly recommended to ensure none of the patterns violates the standards.									
Name of the pattern	Relevant to Usable Security		Effectively Manages the trade-off			Compliance with the standards and best practices			Decision	Additional Recommendations
	Y	N	Y	N	Y/ N	Y	N	Y/N	☐ Accept	1. An addition of Target users to the Pattern will be good such as developers, interface designers, or even end users.

2. The affected sub characteristics can also include *efficiency in use* |
| Data Deletion Pattern | Y | | Y | | | Y | | | | |

Fig. 3. Data deletion pattern review checklist

- **Stage 3:** Involved addition of this pattern to the catalog we are maintaining for dissemination and reuse by other developers.

5   Discussion

The presentation of the methodology during the workshop generated a discussion from which we identified the following avenues for future consideration.

- *Evaluation of instruments for identification of the usable security problem*: There is a need to evaluate different instruments that can help the security and usability experts in identifying the usable security problems with efficacy. For example, some of these instruments include:

- *Surveys*, involving end-users' feedback and qualitative assessment of the problems faced by users while using a security system or service.
- *Heuristic Evaluations*, which are conducted by experts to identify usable security problems due to violations of usability heuristics and security policies.
- *Cognitive Walkthrough*, the security and usability experts inspect the user interfaces of security systems and services by going through a set of tasks and evaluating its understandability, ease of use and learning from the perspective of the targeted population.
- *Contextual Inquiry,* that consists of observing services and systems in use within the context of participants' daily activities and asking for explanations as interesting events arise (security problems, usability problems, comments from users)
- *Semi-structured interviews,* online or on-site with the users of security systems and services. The interviews would be focused on specific usability problems arising from security implementations.
- *Use of tools*, within a lab, the users can be recruited to use security systems and services in a controlled environment. The human system interactions can be recorded using specialized tools like *Morae* or Observer *XT*.

- *Adding quantitative aspects to the methodology*: One dimension that needs further investigation is the addition of a quantitative method in the selection of the best implementations while documenting patterns. As stated in Sect. 3, the methodology considers only the qualitative aspects (expertise of professionals) in the selection of best implementations, therefore, considering the quantitative aspects will support the security and usability experts in selecting the best implementations for identifying and documenting new patterns. A quantitative methodology would also require a set of metrics to assist the identification of best implementations, for example, NUC (number of user complaints) is one such metric that can help in determining the best implementations from the user perspective. The lesser is the NUC, the better is the implementation from the user point of view. However, there is a need to identify a set of these metrics and incorporate their values by assigning weights to come up with a final valuation of the implementations quantitively. This valuation can be used by experts in the selection of the best implementations addressing the usable security problem under consideration.
- *Assessing the across system properties perspective*: Bouzekri *et al.*, presented their work on "Characterizing Sets of Systems: Across-Systems Properties and their Representation" during IFIP WG 13.2 & WG 13.5 Workshop at INTERACT 2019, an interesting aspect to consider from the perspective of our work is the effect of within systems and across system properties on the identified patterns. Considering the across system properties perspective, an important question to address is, do we need different patterns addressing the same usable security problem but requiring different solutions due to the nature of the context in which these systems are deployed?
- *Formalizing the process of selection of experts for review*: To have a set of experts for validation of the identified patterns, the work presented by Larusdottir and Kyas during the workshop identifies a mechanism that can be incorporated for selecting the right set of people for performing a validation job. The authors presented their work

related to the selection of an agile team for a developing development task. However, learning from their approach can be useful in formalizing the process of selection of experts.

6 Conclusion

Inter-dependencies and trade-offs between security and usability need to be approached strategically. The three-stage methodology presented in this paper is an attempt in this regard. Efforts need to be put in to develop a framework within the scope of the system development life cycle (SDLC) for eliciting the conflicts between security and usability while identifying suitable trade-offs between the two. The use of patterns can also be influential in documenting the outcomes of employing such frameworks. Patterns can assist also assist in improved communication between various segments working on the project more precisely the security and usability teams.

Additionally, the use of patterns does not only assist the developers within the organizational setting but also free-lancers in assessing the usability of their security options and vice versa. Furthermore, one pattern only solves one problem in a particular context of usage; therefore, an entire catalog of usable security patterns is required just like the user interface patterns catalog. The development of such a catalog is a time-consuming process and requires community-level efforts, therefore, we intend to present our proposal of using patterns and the methodology for identifying patterns to participants of the Human-Centered Software Engineering and HCI community for their feedback and participation in the development of the usable security patterns catalog.

Acknowledgment. The first author wishes to thank Professor Ahmed Seffah for his feedback during the initial phases of this research.

References

1. Naqvi, B., Seffah, A.: A methodology for aligning usability and security in systems and services. In: 2018 3rd International Conference on Information Systems Engineering, pp. 61–66 (2018)
2. Garfinkel, S., Lipford, H.R.: Usable Security History, Themes, and Challenges. Morgan and Claypool, New York (2014)
3. Whitten, A., Tygar, J.D.: Usability of security: a case study. School of Computing Science, Carnegie Mellon University. Rep. Technical Report CMU-CS-98-155 (1998)
4. Caputo, D.D., et al.: Barriers to usable security? Three organizational case studies. IEEE Secur. Priv. **14**(5), 22–32 (2016)
5. Garg, H., Choudhury, T., Kumar, P., Sabitha, S.: Comparison between significance of usability and security in HCI. In: 2017 3rd International Conference on Computational Intelligence Communication Technology (CICT), pp. 1–4 (2017)
6. Kulyk, O., Neumann, S., Budurushi, J., Volkamer, M.: Nothing comes for free: how much usability can you sacrifice for security? IEEE Secur. Priv. **15**(3), 24–29 (2017)
7. Sasse, M.A., Smith, M., Herley, C., Lipford, H., Vaniea, K.: Debunking security-usability tradeoff myths. IEEE Secur. Priv. **14**(5), 33–39 (2016)

8. Cranor, L.F., Buchler, N.: Better together: usability and security go hand in hand. IEEE Secur. Priv. **12**(6), 89–93 (2014)
9. Cranor, L., Garfinkel, S.: Security and Usability. O'Reilly Media, Inc., Sebastopol (2005)
10. Alexander, C., Ishikawa, S., Silverstein, M.: A Pattern Language. Oxford University Press, Oxford (1977)
11. Tidwell, J.: Designing Interfaces. O'Reilly Media, Inc., Sebastopol (2005)
12. Welie, M.V.: Patterns in interaction design (2008). https://www.welie.com/patterns/
13. Ferreira, A., Rusu, C., Roncagliolo, S.: Usability and security patterns. In: 2nd International Conference on Advances in Computer-Human Interaction, pp. 301–305 (2009)
14. Garfinkel, S., Miller, R.C.: Patterns for aligning security and usability. In: Symposium on Usable Privacy and Security (SOUPS) (2005). https://cups.cs.cmu.edu/soups/2005/2005posters/13-garfinkel.pdf
15. Munoz-Arega, J., et al.: A methodology for designing information security feedback based on user interact patterns. Adv. Eng. Softw. **40**(2009), 1231–1241 (2009)
16. Naqvi, B., Seffah, A.: Interdependencies, conflicts and trade-offs between security and usability: why and how should we engineer them? In: Moallem, A. (ed.) HCII 2019. LNCS, vol. 11594, pp. 314–324. Springer, Cham (2019). https://doi.org/10.1007/978-3-030-22351-9_21
17. Mor, Y., Winters, N., Warburton, S.: Participatory patterns workshops resource kit. Version 2.1 (2010). https://hal.archives-ouvertes.fr/hal-00593108/document
18. Sophos: Security threat report (2010). https://www.sophos.com/sophos/docs/eng/papers/sophos-security-threat-report-jan-2010-wpna.pdf
19. Kirlappos, I., Sasse, M.A.: What usable security really means: trusting and engaging users. In: Tryfonas, T., Askoxylakis, I. (eds.) HAS 2014. LNCS, vol. 8533, pp. 69–78. Springer, Cham (2014). https://doi.org/10.1007/978-3-319-07620-1_7

Author Index

Printed in the United States
By Bookmasters